To Mitch,
A good friend,
Pete Coogan
07-07-07

Don't Shoot the Decoys

Don't Shoot the Decoys

Original Stories of Waterfowling Obsession

Doug Larsen
Illustrations by Jim Rataczak

DUCKS UNLIMITED

Book Design: Karen Almand

Published by Ducks Unlimited, Inc.
L. J. Mayeux, President
Julius Wall, Chairman of the Board
D. A. (Don) Young, Executive Vice President

ISBN: 0-9617279-9-3
Published July 2002

Ducks Unlimited, Inc.
The mission of Ducks Unlimited is to fulfill the annual life cycle
needs of North American waterfowl by protecting, enhancing,
restoring, and managing important wetlands and associated
uplands. Since its founding in 1937, DU has raised more than $1.3
billion, which has contributed to the conservation of over 9.4
million acres of prime wildlife habitat in all fifty states, each of
the Canadian provinces, and in key areas of Mexico. In the U.S.
alone, DU has helped to conserve over 2 million acres of waterfowl habitat. Some 900 species of wildlife live and flourish on DU
projects, including many threatened and endangered species.

Library of Congress Cataloging-in-Publication Data

Larsen, Doug, 1966-
  Don't shoot the decoys : original stories of waterfowling obsession /
  Doug Larsen ; illustrations by Jim Rataczak.
    p. cm.
  ISBN 0-9617279-9-3 (alk. paper)
  1. Waterfowl shooting--Anecdotes. I. Title.
SK331 .L37 2002
799.2'44--dc21
                              2002006332

*For Katie, who displays endless patience
during the duck season and through the year*

CALL TO ACTION

The success of Ducks Unlimited hinges upon each member's personal involvement in the conservation of North America's wetlands and waterfowl. You can help Ducks Unlimited meet its conservation goals by volunteering your time, energy, and resources; by participating in our conservation programs; and by encouraging others to do the same. To learn more about how you can make a difference for the ducks, call 1-800-45-DUCKS.

TABLE OF CONTENTS

ACKNOWLEDGEMENTS

Thanks to Ducks Unlimited, whose involvement with me was the equivalent of hunting a new spot with nothing to go on but a few rumors and a map scrawled on the back of a cocktail napkin.

Thanks to Charlie Johnson. He was in the blind a lot in the early days.

INTRODUCTION

Another parent told me a story recently about a child going into a first-grade class on the very first day of school at a grade school near my home. First graders are quite young, most just six or barely seven. While there is excitement on that first day, many are apprehensive about being away from home and away from the security of their surroundings for a full day for the first time. It seems that in this particular class, the experienced teacher was well aware of this, and each year on the first day she gradually introduces the children into their new roles as full-time students. So instead of starting the lesson plans immediately, she began the day with some fun and music. As the teacher told the children about her plan to play some songs, she removed a record album from its poster board sleeve and frail paper dustcover, and began to place it on the turntable of her portable phonograph. At this point, one of the more precocious boys in the class spoke up. He pointed at the phonograph record and exclaimed, "That's the biggest compact disc I've ever seen!"

So it is in these times of changing technologies. It seems that as fast as we get caught up with the technology that tries to stampede us daily, there is another technology just behind it waiting to charge forward and change things further. Everywhere we are making the part smaller, the pace faster, or the widget better. I guess I'm just a traditionalist in many ways, but I still insist that I'd rather crank down the truck window with a proper handle instead of pushing an electric button, and I'd rather go inside the restaurant than talk to a speaker. But it is hard for me to frame in my mind that many of today's kids have never seen a phonograph record and have no appreciation of black-and-white television programs. The latest craze, meanwhile, is for the kids in my neighborhood to pump and glide sleek aluminum scooters up and down the street. These scooters, I'm told by the kids on my block, are "the greatest new thing." These same kids are oblivious of the fact that a very similar version of that type of scooter has been around for years, and they might still see Opie Taylor or the Beaver riding one through their respective neighborhoods...if they were willing to tune in to even a little black-and-white television, and the Beaver instead of Beavis in the first place.

DVD seems to be the current movie and musical technological rage, and this is frightening to me since I'm still at least one technology behind and still cannot program the VCR to tape the outdoor shows when I'd rather be outdoors. Until it was explained to me, I thought DVD had something to do with a government agency that controlled the spread of venereal disease. If you want to scroll back three or four technologies, you may visit my basement, where I still have a few eight-track tapes squirreled away in case the Climax Blues Band or the Doobie Brothers ever stage a comeback. While I have the eight-tracks, I have lost track of the Chevy Nova that had the eight-track player in it.

✦ ✦ ✦

Duck hunting has been swept along in the technological tidal wave along with everything else around us. Biologists can now routinely track migratory birds with tiny radio transmitters, and Internet sites allow even the amateur to find migrating ducks and geese on radar from the comforts of a home office. Hunting licenses are purchased on line, and today's young hunter has not likely ever bought a box of shotgun shells over the counter of a general store. From a historical perspective, the teenagers and youngsters that we are hopefully taking to the marshes and rivers and rice fields and timber in the present seasons have very likely never shot a lead-loaded shotgun shell at waterfowl, and it hasn't been an option to them in their lifetimes. Has it really been twenty years or so ago since we switched to steel, or now to bismuth or tungsten or some of the other heavy metals that are now available to us? I suppose it has. Many of today's kids have never worn a canvas hunting coat or even rubber waders in this age of Gore-Tex and neoprene and Windstopper fleece.

If you had told me even ten years ago that my favorite duck call would be made from acrylic, I would have called you a heretic. I would have told you that acrylic is for latex house paint, and real duck calls are supposed to be turned out of wood. But as Dustin Hoffman was told in *The Graduate*, the future was and is in plastics. Guess what calls I have swinging around my neck during the season? One made of clear plastic and the other of clear acrylic. I don't have warm and fuzzy feelings about either call; in fact, they both look a little bit like veterinary syringes. But both calls work better than any others I've tried recently, wood included, so I blow my plastic call and raise my truck window with the electric button. I'm adapting.

Many of us in our thirties and forties and even fifties who have been in the ducking business for any length of time would be hard pressed finding someone to talk to who even remembers live decoys, much less someone who has actually hunted over them, even though we'd love to hear about it. About as many old-timers would recall the days of the twenty-five-duck limit, and that seems like such a big number today. But live decoys and big bags were commonplace less than 100 years ago, and both practices have gone the way of tires with inner tubes and the gramophone in a relatively short period of time.

Time passes, but the allure of duck hunting continues to be passed from generation to generation. Historians trace some of the very earliest references to duck hunting to the walls of King Tutankhamen's tomb. How fascinating that for centuries, since the time of the pyramids and the pharaohs and their hounds, men have suffered restless nights because they were too excited to really sleep before greeting the dawn of a duck hunting day. Yet today, in an age when I could send a color picture of a flock of ducks to someone in Cairo in seconds with the click of a button, outdoorsmen still pause at the whistle of wings overhead, or stop to gaze and wonder at a skein of geese traveling across the horizon near dusk. The casual observer might make the mistake of thinking that we, as hunters, are looking at those birds because we are awed by their ability to fly. But I like to think that it is not flight so much as it is freedom. We don't look on in wonderment at a vapor trail as it hangs in the sky. Flight in the early twenty-first century is mundane, and airplanes are merely buses traveling miles above the earth. It is the freedom and connection to wild places that binds us to the birds.

It is my love for duck hunting and all things related to ducks and their pursuit that inspired me to write these twenty stories, and I'm being quite honest in stating that—for me personally—duck shooting isn't about shooting ducks, though that is the crux of it. Think back to your own experiences in the marsh; the part you remember is not the instant when the guns go off. The freeze-frame is the very second before the guns go off. That is what we take with us. That is what sticks in our memories. It is the cusp of the actual shooting—or the chill of a morning marsh, dog noses on windows, or the cupped wings of a flock of sleek puddle ducks or blocky divers coming to decoys—that excites me about the sport and the passion and the lifestyle of a duck hunter. Just plain being out there is a huge part of the whole, and many of us hunt ducks on a lot of days when the chances of actually shooting a bird are very, very slim.

But chasing ducks also includes the getting there, and the coming home. It is long truck rides with friends and damp dogs, pumpguns that short shuck, tangleproof decoy lines that tangle, and boat trailer wiring that blinks when wet. It is a simple dinner of grilled mallards and a cold beer on an impossibly hot July evening that remind us that autumn is not really too far away, or the laughter from a boy as he rolls in the grass with a new black puppy, and the promise that lies in both the puppy and the boy. It is handing down wellworn guns and jackets within a duck hunting family and borrowing dry socks for the ride home. It is the reliving and retelling, and a band appearing unexpectedly on the leg of the only duck you shot after staying alone in your blind until late in the afternoon.

It may also be that duck hunting for many of us is a chance to relive our own youths for at least a small part of each year. We are able to motor away from the dock of ennui and commitment that includes, but is not limited to, commuting, middle management, and an overdue mortgage payment. If we are truly lucky, we can get out of the cellular phone coverage area to sit in a fort, much like those we built in the yard with our friends as kids.

I still love that I get a very childlike rush when I come home from my workday and find a box from Cabela's or Herter's or Mack's Prairie Wings on my front porch. I love to pull new decoys from the box, place them on my lawn, and walk back ten or fifteen paces to eyeball them from a distance. I love a sport that touches grown men so deeply that they'll play hooky from their careers for just one blasting weather day over a diver spread, or they'll walk the razor's edge of the very sanctity of their marriage to get under mallards that are working a cut cornfield. I love that I can call and arrange a "play date" with grown men who are excited about me picking them up at their houses at three-thirty or four o'clock in the black dark of morning. I look forward to sharing the last of the coffee with them, and to patting them on the back when they make a double or when their dogs make them proud. And there are few things that swell my chest more than hearing one of them say "nice shot," knowing that he really means it.

I have been very fortunate that through my years of duck hunting I have been able to sample some shooting in some far-off lands. I have made many shooting trips to Argentina, hunted ducks in the marshes of Mexico and on the lagoons of Uruguay, and even slept under reindeer skins in tented duck camps in Siberia. While I have enjoyed the travel and shooting experiences I have had abroad and would recommend many of them, most of the basis for what you'll find in this book is from closer to home. While on any given day the duck shooting in Argentina or Mexico will be better than what I might find in Ohio or Minnesota, where I was raised, there is something about the familiar that gives it more meaning, and something about suffering the slow days close to home that make the really good days stand out even more vividly.

As we look to duck hunting's future, there is still much to be done to ensure that we are able to carry North America's fragile wetland resources and waterfowl populations into the next decades of this new century, and if we aren't careful, we'll have nothing left but our own home movies of the good old days, which we can transfer onto DVD. Potholes and northern nesting areas continue to disappear at an alarming rate and ducks and geese face new pressures from farming practices and development at the southern end of their annual journey that they did not face just a few years ago. Like all problems, to keep ducks and good duck country on the right track, it will take our interest, time, and money. It is up to those of us who live and love duck hunting to make a contribution, whether we hunt mallards in swathed grain near Moose Jaw, or gadwalls in flooded rice near Bayou Meto. Ducks and geese are truly the movable feast, available to all of us at each end of the flyways and at every spot along the map in between where men and boys—and, increasingly, girls—wait with camouflage and boats and dogs and cameras and shotguns to witness the miracle of the migration each year. Sustaining this tradition for our children and involving the next generation not only teaches them that we care, but also, by example, teaches them how to care. In the long haul, a legacy rich in waterfowl, marshes, and open spaces will be an inheritance far more valuable to our kids than shares of a computer company, a bond portfolio, or the Wedgwood china.

RATACZAK Ⓒ '01

Chapter One

MOVABLE HEADS

I was hunting alone last week, and after a fairly satisfying morning, despite a cloudless sky, decided it was time to wrap up the decoys and get on home. Normally, I'm hesitant to rush into the picking up of decoys, preferring to stand in the open for several minutes drinking the last of the coffee. Or I'll walk around the blind or sit outside it, daring any last trading bird to make a move. As most of us know, these acts often bring some type of action. The simple process of unloading a gun and the sound of zipping a gun case are usually enough to have any self-respecting duck within three counties charging for the decoys.

On this day, however, there was to be none of that. My action was early, in the first hour of the day, when there was a busy morning flight that started well before shooting time. But now at midmorning, the temperature was unusually warm, I was down to shirtsleeves, and the sun was beating down like Dr. Evil's death ray. There wasn't a bird in the sky of any type. I'm usually a stone-cold pessimist on these kinds

1

of days, and curse the weather, the duck gods, the weather reporters, global warming, and that El Niño kid. I resent the wrapping and stowing and rowing that picking up a hundred or so decoys entails.

But as they say, a funny thing happened on the way to the dance. As I got started, having resigned myself to the fact that the shooting was over, I actually found that I was relieved not to feel like I was leaving too early, missing the chance to decoy just one more bird. For the first time in years, I was satisfied and enjoying picking up. It was like I had emerged from some twelve-step program for duck hunters. I was at peace.

In wrapping my decoys, a collection of twenty-odd years worth of hunting ducks, I also took the time to reflect on where some of these decoys had come from, and on the little stories behind them. Decoys are vitally important to the duck hunter. They are the foot in the door, the sales force, and the first impression. Of course, a bunch of my decoys are just part of the nameless, faceless mass of a decoy spread, just faces in the crowd. Some are plastic mallard decoys, distinguished only by one kind of cord or another, a clip on the keel, a lead strap, or a mushroom anchor. Older decoys have paint scraped from the side of the body or the head from rubbing other decoys in transit, or from being tossed in and out of the boat countless times.

Others, though, are more recognizable. I came across a bluebill decoy that had been my grandfather's. It isn't cork, or carved wood, and while that might make the history seem more rich, this decoy still has a patina of its own. This one rubber decoy, with a few stray shot lodged in the body and a red valve stem sticking out of its backside, is marked along the keel with my grandfather's name in heavy black pen. He was gone long before I was able to share a blind with him, and I still recall the day when my grandmother pointed me to her garage to "take whatever might be of use." That decoy surely floated the wild rice lakes of northern Minnesota during duck hunting's heyday. Boats were wooden then, clothes were wool, and shot was lead, and I imagine this decoy riding with others in the green chop of a hidden bay, on a day when the sky was dark and the water was the color of gunmetal. I imagine my grandfather picking out a drake, as bluebills and redheads buzz the spread. His old pumpgun barks, and he shucks paper empties onto the floor of a point blind—heady stuff to be dreaming on this balmy day.

Another bluebill in my set is a hard plastic decoy that is easily recognizable by a glass eye and a very formal body style. Standing out like a regal gentleman in the soup line of my other pedestrian diving duck decoys, this was the first diver I bought as a kid. I recall buying the drake, along with a hen that is no longer with me, at a hardware store in rural Minnesota. This pair of decoys was bought with money saved from walking bean fields. More modern farming and sprayed chemicals have largely replaced "walking the beans," as the job was titled, but for a generation of kids, summers of going up and down the rows of beans, pulling out volunteer cornstalks and thistles, was a vocation that provided some pocket money. While much of this money was squandered on root beer and slingshots and yo-yos—the spoils of youth—I remember the pride I felt in displaying those decoys on the bedroom dresser before the hunting season. Like my Farrah Fawcett poster, they were an important element of my interior decorating, but they were also part of the effort to add color to my spread, something that had been suggested by a sage writer in one of the outdoor magazines I pored through. Of course, in those days my "spread" consisted of eight mallard decoys and a burlap sack.

As I continued to wrap and row, and place decoys behind me in the bow of my little boat, I came to another plastic decoy, and while I cleared a healthy portion of pondweed and snails from its anchor, it occurred to me that this big white cork block was one of a dozen goldeneye decoys I had once hunted over, the sole survivor salvaged from the blizzard of 1991. That year I had permission to hunt with several friends on a lake near my home in Minnesota. It wasn't the most productive duck lake, but it was close by and easy to hunt for an hour or two before work, and we had a comfortable point blind for weekend hunts.

Saturday morning before the storm that year, the shooting had been good, especially by our standards for this little lake, and the diving ducks came to the decoys with abandon. For a morning, we were living a Gordon MacQuarrie story and loving it. Since the wind was building, and even stronger weather was forecast for the following morning, we decided to leave the decoys out overnight, something we never did in those days. But it was decided by all involved that we should go home to warm up and skip the picking up on this day. After all, we'd be back in the blind the next morning.

But we never made it back to the blind on Sunday. By dawn, the storm was so fierce, and the snow so deep, that we didn't make it out of our houses that day, or for the three days following that Halloween blizzard. Thirty-seven inches of windblown snow had fallen by Tuesday. On Wednesday, we were at our little lake on snowmobiles. Easily able to walk on the ice that had formed in three days, we spent the day reclaiming what we could find of our spread. We cut decoys out with chain saws and chopped them out with ice spuds, then piled them on a trailer to take to a nearby pole barn to thaw. Later, as the heat and smell of kerosene heaters filled the barn air, the great ovals of ice that surrounded each decoy began to drip away. We left the decoys on the dirt floor to melt like the witch from the *Wizard of Oz*.

Many, many decoys were lost that weekend, never to be seen again—even in the spring thaw. How only this single whistler survived, I cannot recall, but what a pleasure to have it with me now to bring back the memories of that ferocious weekend storm.

Other decoys in my spread I remember by the dozen, like the big water-keeled mallards I bought cheaply from a casual friend who was at the time wrestling with a divorce. In need of ready cash, he was cleaning out the garage, and things did not go well for him, I heard later. I usually don't stop to think about him until I pick up the first of these water-keels, and as a stream of water rushes over my arm and lap, I recall that I promised myself to fill these keels at the end of last season and I wonder if my friend ever got over the pain of that parting. I'd like to think that he's happy, maybe remarried by now and perhaps even duck hunting again.

I get out of the boat, waving at a hatch of gnats that has balled up around my head in the warm air. Wading into the shallowest part of the decoy spread, I begin to wind up short-corded mallard decoys at a steady pace, flipping each into the boat as I go. While wading with the aluminum skiff, I keep it near me, my elbow tucked into the prow. I chuckle almost out loud now as I come to the decoys my witty friend Charlie has dubbed the cross dressers, two mallard blocks of the type that, like my daughter's Barbie dolls, have movable heads. What a concept that was! Sometime back, I was hooked by the notion that my spread would be very lifelike with some heads turned this way and others that. I knew wary mallards would look down from above and feel as secure as if they'd just seen their therapist if they saw these blocks, looking so casual and so at ease. Looking back now, I must have made too big a deal of this feature, as one day Charlie fitted the head of a drake to the body of a hen, and the head of a hen to the body of a drake. He then placed both off to the side of the decoy rig. By luck or happenstance, the day he did this the ducks decoyed beautifully, and after the hunt he opined that the dead mallards and gadwalls in our blind did not seem to notice the pair of unisex decoys. I was shocked beyond comment at the time, and could not believe we had gotten our shooting, given this serious breach of realism. Now, more than twelve years later, I refuse to change those two decoys back to their proper selves. Instead they are placed out as a pair and have become a reference point in the spread. "Mark left, ten o'clock, low over the cross-dressers."

Almost done now, the boat brimming with decoys, I reflect that the last hour or so has been an inspirational trip down my duck hunting memory lane. I pity those hunters who pass-shoot their ducks, or jump potholes to get shooting, or those permanent-blind hunters in the South, who often hunt huge spreads of a thousand decoys or more. While I'd like to see a set like that someday, surely a thousand decoys must be a crowd, and though I'm sure the big, big spreads are effective, it must be tough to find old friends and memories like I have with me here.

Chapter Two

CARPET SLIPPERS

Although there are still hunters who do things the hard way, if you talk to enough duck hunters and spend time reading the popular hunting press, it seems that things have gotten pretty cushy for a lot of waterfowlers as we collectively move through the early part of the new century. I still know some hardy duck chasers with the kind of secretive spirit that trout fishermen often possess—guys who think nothing of a two- or three-mile walk into a secluded marsh or a little beaver pond. But these hunters seem to be fewer and farther between, these days. Those who still have the "out there" spirit may no longer hump a dozen cork decoys to their spot on their backs. They find the spot with a satellite map, mark it with global positioning, and—more often than not—have one of those four-wheeled ATVs to get them, along with four- or five-dozen plastic decoys and the rest of their stuff, where they need to be in safety and comfort. The rest of us are content with our public marshes, or our leases, and we are often just trying to get ducks before they get to the other guy.

I'm as guilty as anyone. I love a comfortable duck blind as much as anybody, and on a day when the wind is whipping up a chop and the thermometer shows a number about like my dog's IQ score, there is nothing like a ride to my spot in a big warm American truck, a little blind heater, and my trusty thermos bottle to make the morning bearable. But hasn't the need for comfort gotten a little out of hand?

I saw a photo the other day of a duck blind that was an enormous sunken pit on a river sandbar. The guys who hunted it had a full-blown kitchen in this thing, with a stove and hot and cold running water, along with hot and cold running Labradors. These guys claimed to have prepared grilled cheese sandwiches, pancakes, pheasant breasts, and even fried fish fillets for lunch. One of the guys interviewed in the article under the picture said he had a good recipe for French toast too. I'd hate to be the one holding the sticky Aunt Jemima syrup bottle when the gadwalls come to call.

I have seen houseboat blinds with privies, kitchens, and roofs that have been converted into shooting decks. On some of them, the hunters laze about in heated comfort and watch sports on television, and are summoned to the roof by the lookout only when birds approach. I assume that at least some of the ducks have manners enough to arrive only during commercial time-outs. I can only imagine some of what goes on in these floating lodges. "Harry, you take the ducks on the left as they decoy, but watch out you don't shoot low if the birds cross near the satellite dish."

I have seen and been in some of the big, big floating blinds on lakes and reservoirs in the South, and many of them are very plush as well. Guides ride as many as six or eight sports out to these enormous floating blinds that occupy a prime point or pass. After parking the boat in a special garage under the blind, guides settle in to call ducks, make coffee, and tidy things up. Guides are not bothered with the putting out of decoys, as these are left out for the season. They do run serious spreads of decoys from these large floating affairs—as many as 1,000. It is worth the trip to one of these outfits just to see the decoy spread—or, with 1,000 decoys and a blind that big, you could wait for the photos, as I'm sure the spy cameras will spot them on the next satellite pass.

Then there are private duck clubs where well-heeled gunners pad about the hallways in carpet slippers, drinks in hand. After sleeping the sound sleep of gundogs each evening, the "old sports" are awakened each morning by a member of the white-jacketed staff who knocks politely and delivers fresh coffee and croissants. Duck shooters at many old-line private clubs struggle to get out of bed, reluctant to leave their eider down comforters and crisp bedding. But they persevere, and after breakfast the old gents shuffle off to blinds where their punters or boatmen direct them to the duck shooting at hand. Owing to the huge lands or marshes held exclusively for the club and its members, the hunting is usually fabulous, and gin rummy (and gin drinking) typically follow each morning's duck "shooting." Meanwhile, the staff cleans the day's spoils and retrieves fine vintages from club cellars prior to the evening feast.

A good friend of mine called me from the airport after his experience at one of the old money clubs in the northeast a season or two ago. He was rushing through the airport on the way home and did not have the time to relay the whole story. "I'll tell you all about it when I get home," he said. Then he added, "But I can tell you they had paintings on the walls and white furniture in the clubhouse. Imagine that, white furniture in a duck club for Chrissakes!" Certainly a far cry from the experiences a lot of us are used to, ranging from sneaking a muddy dog into a reputable motel to old nudie posters and ammunition calendars that decorate the more out-of-the-way duck lodges and duck shacks of many regions.

Even the average duck boat has vastly improved, and now the brochures you find on the counters at these big sports shows held in convention centers list hunting boats with amenities. I thought travel trailers and fine hotels were the only things that offered amenities. The new breed of duck rigs offers a selection of several different camouflage paint

schemes from the factory, along with waterproof, bass-boat-like carpet; dry storage; dog ladders; shell trays; cup holders; blinds that fold up and fold down in seconds; running lights; work lights; and twelve-volt receptacles for heaters or anything that needs power. Jacques Cousteau didn't have many of the options available on today's duck boats onboard the *Calypso*. If you hunt on the water exclusively, and you don't object to a little financing, you can manage to get things pretty comfy for yourself in a duck boat these days too.

But the world of waterfowling hasn't all turned to carpeted boats and carpet slippers just yet. I recently met a group of guys who are still doing it the hard way, and whether duck hunting to you is sitting on a bucket in the mud or having Charles press your shooting britches at the club, or something in between, you have to give these guys credit for clinging to tradition. They call themselves the Mighty Layout Boys, and they are a little group of men who learned layout shooting by competing for several seasons with an old market hunter in Michigan. For more than twenty years the

Mighty Layout Boys have continued the market gunner's tradition of lying alone in a little slip of a boat, often in icy water, rolling waves, and treacherous conditions, with the express purpose of shooting diving ducks.

Diving duck aficionados are a special breed in the first place, and the serious diver specialist thrives on rough weather, rough water, and the appeal of making the best of things with scouting, guts, skill, and good equipment. Diver duck hunting is like black-and-white television: everything appears in shades of gray. It has its own monochromatic appeal, and it is plenty good if you don't try to compare it to color.

But taking risks to kill ducks may have been the kind of thing you did if you were hunting back in the early days of the twentieth century, when the market was paying a dollar per canvasback. Back then, a take of eighty or more big ducks on a given day was a possibility, and working outdoorsmen built boats, carved decoys, and shot ducks for the same reason coal miners mined coal. Killing ducks paid the bills. How many of us today can say that we take some chances—not stupid ones; I'm not promoting recklessness—in pursuit of our sport? The fact is, as equipment, weather prediction, boat and motor reliability, and clothing improve, we all push the envelope a little less. Fewer and fewer of us are willing to go through the motions for the chance at shooting just one canvasback or a few other flavors of diving ducks in an outing. Those who spend any time in good-sized duck boats know how dangerous conditions can get, and crossing a big body of water with a partner, decoys, a dog, and all kinds of gear in the dark is oftentimes enough of a challenge.

Now imagine strapping a little pumpkin-seed-shaped boat across the bow of a skiff, and filling the boat with 700 pounds of homemade cork decoys, and another 100 or so pounds of anchors and gear. Attached to the stern is a big wheel that looks like one of those hand-cranked air raid sirens from a vintage war movie, and it plays out and retrieves the long lines to which decoys are fastened. Once you and your layout partner have the little kayak-like boat anchored at both ends and surrounded by 100 or 200 decoys, imagine an open-water transfer from the big boat to the little layout in the dark. I have a hard time coming to grips with stepping out of a perfectly good twenty-foot skiff into a rolling, bobbing layout boat. I have this reoccurring image of the circus act where the bear balances on the big colored ball, only the bear is good at it. But getting into the boat is just the beginning.

With the exception of a few layout boats that were designed to accommodate two men, most layouts are home-built, one-hunter affairs. If you are not familiar with this style of shooting, this is what you do: You lie on your back, with your feet splayed out, your heels touching, and your head just peeking out of the boat. To shoot, you must brace your feet and lift yourself by bending at the waist while concentrating on rising to shoot at incoming birds. Most of us assume this position only on the couch at home and rise only to point the remote. Try this at-home self-test. Next time you need to pull the trigger on the channel changer, pretend your television is a canvasback crossing low over the decoys and that your couch is on rollers. Imagine how well you'd score. After meeting these layout boat guys, I have been thinking about devising a sporting clays station to simulate layout shooting. You would have to shoot at low incoming targets while reclining on an old chaise longue that has been placed on top of a spongy king-size mattress. As you called for your target, the trap boy would jump up and down behind you, activating the rolling wave feature of the mattress. And you thought "springing teal" were difficult.

What about the camaraderie that we all enjoy while sitting in our blinds, shooting the breeze between flights of birds— talking sports, politics, hunting, or family while waiting for a flight of stragglers? None of that happens for the layout crew. You lie alone in your boat, scanning the waves and the skies, with nobody to talk to but the decoys. Need to relieve yourself? You should have gone before you took that long last step out of the tender boat. Want a nice hot cup of java to cut the chill from the spray that is washing across the deck and trickling down your neck? Sorry, no room for a thermos in here. But take solace in the knowledge that all layout boats include a sponge as part of their standard "amenity" package. Why the sponge? For bailing, of course. You've got to keep the water out and the boat is too small for a pail.

Even the most experienced layout shooter won't suffer for long, as by its very nature, a stint in a layout only lasts for an hour or so. After an hour, even the most hardy are usually driven to wave for the tender boat by cold, wet, or claustrophobia. Layout partners then trade places, and the man not in shooting position holds the tender boat downwind a half mile or so to keep an eye on his companion—and retrieve him, if necessary—while waiting for his next shift in the little soap dish of a craft.

As tippy, wet, cold, and dangerous as layout gunning can be, it is not ineffective. Far from it. Lying out is lethal on diving ducks, since—like the outlawed sink box—layouts virtually disappear in the water. In fact, in a perfectly designed and functioning boat, the spray skirt or cowling around the cockpit of the boat is adjusted until it keeps water mostly out of the boat and off the hunter, but water from wave action washes continually over the decks, so the boat is hidden both on and virtually in the waves. Most boats are painted in a gray to green camouflage scheme, following a large, rolling pattern reminiscent of World War II torpedo boats and destroyers.

Mark Rongers, one of the leaders of the Mighty Layout Boys, shared a story with me about a layout trip he made in Canada in the early 1990s. His party of five men took a two-man John Kalash layout boat out onto Ontario's Lake Nipissing on a windy day that started out promising and turned almost deadly. Imagine a lake sixty miles long, rolling with huge green waves produced by a straight-line wind in excess of forty miles per hour. After picking up their open-water rig, Mark motored five men and 200 decoys more than three miles in an eighteen-footer with the layout boat in tow. The group made it to shore, but it was a grim, white-knuckle ride. In the layout game, you don't need to be anchored in a shipping lane to feel very exposed, and when you find yourself exposed, it seems Mother Nature is always willing to wait you out.

To be truthful, many state and federal regulations have made it difficult for layout shooters to ply their trade, as modern migratory bird regulations seek to protect ducks that are resting in open water. This is perhaps as it should be, and many agree that migrating divers deserve a break from harassment while on big bodies of water. Still, layouts are effective even with these laws in place, and many of the northern states allow open-water shooting, which helps to keep the lore of the layout rigs alive.

Entrenched so firmly in a sport virtually within a sport, and influenced by traditions at least a century old—like making tight boats and carving big, hardy cork decoys—what was the next step for the Mighty Layout Boys? Naturally, they did what any modern traditionalist must do: They started their own Internet Web site, so they could

share their stories with the rest of us. Look for them at www.
mightylayoutboys.com.

WET CEMENT

L et me state for the record that I have a wonderful father. He was a great dad to my siblings and me when we were children, and he continues to be a helpful parent to me in my adult life. These days, on the verge of retirement, Dad has also settled comfortably into the role of the bespectacled, doting grandfather to my kids, but he's the kind of grandpa who's not afraid to jump in the autumn leaf pile or swing a little himself when he's with the kids at the playground. He has logged forty-plus years of a fine and happy marriage to my mother, and it speaks volumes about his character that he recently carefully cut the wedding ring my mother gave him from his finger with a hacksaw blade. He hadn't removed his wedding ring since they were first married, and it was so tight it had started to render his ring finger numb. After Dad removed his own ring, worn paper-thin with age, he replaced it with the wedding ring his father had worn his entire married life.

I find myself looking back across the span that was my adolescence more and more as I age, and I guess that's natural.

As I look back, I'm now more able to realize that my father spent the vast majority of his working life busting the tip off his pick for his children. While ultimately all of his grown kids went different directions, I know we'd all like to believe that we are well adjusted, productive adults because our father—or, more accurately, both our parents—achieved the delicate balance of paying attention to us, which the parenting gurus call "quality time" these days, while giving us metered independence. But my dad, especially, slipped me enough figurative rope that I always had the option of hanging myself if I didn't make the smart or moral or safe choice. I came running home more than once after finding myself swinging from a rope of my own knotting, and he always welcomed me back to the nest. Somewhere in the process I learned one lesson or another. Anyway, I'd be more than content to have someone refer to me as a "chip off the old block," even though you don't hear that expression much anymore.

While my passion has always been for the outdoors, and specifically for marshes and duck hunting, hunting was just not Dad's bag. A strong, quiet man with huge hands and bright eyes, he came from rugged Danish farm stock. Dad was raised on the family farm in the Midwest, and my theory on farmers and farmers' children is that—because they grow up tied to the outdoors and are so reliant on the cycles of weather and growing seasons and light—they never develop the passion to be outside. To many of them, hunting or fishing is just another way of collecting food. There is no element

22

of sport. Farmers often see the outdoors as an adversary. Few learn to feel the release from an escape to the outdoors, since for many it is part of the struggle in their everyday lives.

Like many rural kids, my dad moved away from the farm after college, and he and my mother raised three children in a slate blue ranch house with an attached garage on a long shady block in the suburbs of Minneapolis, where I spent most of my youth. Dad and I went fishing on occasion, and he tried to lure me into golf early, suggesting that it would be a good game to know how to play in my adult life. At fifteen, I knew everything there was to know about everything, so I resisted golf completely, calling it a wimpy game. I had birds to shoot and fish to catch, and couldn't be bothered with pasture pool. These days I spend virtually each summer Saturday getting fleeced by my friends at the wimpy game, and I wish I had played more golf and learned the game when I was young. I've just chalked the endless string of $10 Nassau losses up to another time when I should have listened to my dad. In my teenage years when I should have been forming a lasting relationship with my father, I misspent much of my time seining minnows for bait, trout fishing, walking roadside ditches for pheasants, and pothole hunting ducks just outside of town. Meanwhile, my father was putting food on the table, taking care of our house and small yard, and pouring concrete in his spare time.

I hunted with my dad only once, on the opening day of pheasant season in Minnesota, when I was thirteen. I'm sure he could not have cared less, but I assume he finally gave in to my nagging and reminding because he had reached the stage where it was easier just to walk a few hours carrying a shotgun than to hear about pheasants for another minute. Believe me, he knew the date for the opening day long before it ever rolled around.

I was fresh out of my youth firearms safety class, and on a clear day in Jackson County with a wind that made every cornstalk rustle and the fat pines pulse, my dad and I walked through the windbreak around the family farm. I wore my new canvas shell vest, still stiff and golden colored, with the orange hunter safety patch sewn to the breast. Dad had just pulled on work boots, a John Deere cap, and had a few Federal Cartridge game loads in the pocket of his putty-colored Eisenhower jacket. We walked along side by side, and before long the legs of my blue jeans were soaking wet to the knee as I waded through high grass and thistles. I carried my single-shot 20-gauge in the extremely safe fashion that I had recently learned was called the port-arms carry. I had a full box of ammunition with me, twenty-four carefully placed shotshells in my vest, and one in the gun.

We did not have a bird dog, despite the advice of the many, many magazines I had read that suggested that a well-trained dog would aid in our ability to find and retrieve downed birds. However, Tippy, our farm dog—a big collie mix with golf-ball-sized mats of hair hanging from her haunches and her jaw wired shut due to a recent car accident—followed along on my heels. All morning, I tried repeatedly to order Tippy home, as she did not fit into the scheme of the sport as I had envisioned it on opening day. I thought we should have had a thin-boned Irish setter out in front of us, his bell ringing as he bounded through the golden grass, stopping only to point staunchly at the gaudy, long-tailed roosters we would surely find. As it turned out, Dad made the only shot we had at a pheasant, a bird that jumped out from a little triangle of grass between a woodlot and a wire fence, and rose through a stand of trees. As the bird climbed, Dad centered it with one shot from his old, recoil-operated Remington auto, and several feathers floated in the air. On the way down, the rooster bounced rather unceremoniously on the large branches of a mature oak, then landed with what I remember as an undignified thump. From the moment the bird flushed to the time it fell, I remained frozen in the port-arms position, my thumb still on the uncocked hammer of my single-shot gun and my heart racing after the noise of the flush.

Dad retrieved the bird and handed it to me with the happy smirk he still displays to this day. It is a look that pronounces accomplishment in an understated, Nordic way, and it pushes his cheeks up under his eyeglasses and creates little vertical lines in the center of his cheeks. This is a face I see a lot when Dad's golf ball lands on the dry ground just beyond the pond, when the kids say something memorable, or when we arrive at our destination and his shortcut directions have somehow worked.

While I don't remember much of what happened after we got that pheasant, I can still see the blood-red plastic of the empty 12-gauge hull lying in the wet, black earth at my father's feet, and I can still smell the burned powder, swept away by the fall wind.

To return to the subject of Dad and pouring concrete, it is important to note that my father is not a builder or a cement contractor. He has always been a coat-and-tie guy, and through his career he has managed railroad shipping, run a flour mill, and traded grain and commodities. He was a Ward Cleaver who wore a cardigan sweater, shared some tomatoes with the neighbors, and worked nine to five—a briefcase dad who never missed a Little League game, school play, or swimming meet. Win or lose, he was always there to offer his own brand of quiet encouragement. Yet on Saturdays and Sundays he attacked household projects with gusto, possessing as he does remark-able self-taught skills in all the trades, from electrical wiring to carpentry to plumbing. For some strange reason, he has always loved to pour concrete for fun. And it wasn't like we had some huge compound with acres and acres. The slate blue house was not a hobby farm with barns and outbuildings. It was just a modest suburban house on a half-acre lot.

But Dad's idea of a perfect Saturday was to whip up a batch of concrete and pour little spillways underneath the downspouts of the house, or he'd build forms and make a cement platform on which to place the garbage cans. "Easier to mow around them," he'd say.

In my teenage years, I discovered that I had not inherited my father's building skills, and while I fairly coasted through high school, I made very poor grades in shop class. My wooden paper towel holder received a C, a grade I accepted with some relief, since as kitchen aids go, the holder was wobbly and finished in polyurethane varnish that had dried with runs and blobs that made it look almost purposely textured. My second project faired little better: a metal garden trowel that looked like the kind of weapon guards would find hidden on a prison inmate.

Despite my own lack of skills, I still felt welcome to tease Dad about his love for rather permanent construction. He'd just roll his eyes, smirk at me, and shrug it off. But my mother often protected him. On a weekend long ago, I stood with my mother in our blue-and-white wallpapered kitchen late one afternoon, the copper pans hanging from the ceiling casting long shadows on the walls around us. I looked out to see Dad on his knees in the yard, making little sideways swipes with his trowel and putting the finishing touches on a dinner-plate-sized concrete circle around the post that supported our bird feeder. I made a flip comment. Wiping her hands on her apron, my mother looked at me until she was certain that she had fixed my gaze, and said, "Your father is home making the house look nice for all of us, and you should be able to appreciate that the concrete will make that post easier to mow around since you do the lawn mowing, honey. Consider yourself lucky—your dad could be in some bar someplace watching football."

Dad's concrete fixation continued through my teen years, and each weekend in good weather there appeared patios, walkways, an extra parking spot alongside the driveway, sidewalks, birdbaths, and little trim strips of concrete around fence posts and clothes poles on the little lot around the slate blue ranch house. The good news was, Mom was right. The mowing did get easier: there was less and less grass every week as it was replaced by smooth white concrete. Every duck blind I ever built was made from concrete-spattered lumber that I scrounged from the forms that had shaped one of Dad's projects.

Early in Dad's concrete-pouring days—before the portable basketball backboards I now see in many suburban driveways, and during an era I refer to as my Harlem Globetrotter's period—my father once mounted a basketball hoop for me on the roof above the attached garage of the low blue ranch house. He drilled holes in the roof and ran bolts through the rafters to secure it. The backboard and hoop were regulation height, and they were solid. But within hours Dad discovered to his horror that every errant shot that hit the backboard shook the entire house, right down to the good china, and the first afternoon of free throw shooting had given everyone in the place a tic. Nobody in the family could read or eat or relax. Everyone agonized about the next free throw to slap the rim, and then cringed at the vibration that followed.

By the following Saturday my dad, sick of being held hostage in his own home by games of "round the world," had

acquired a piece of steel pipe from some friend at a railway yard, and had welded the backboard and hoop to it. I seem to recall the pipe was about twenty feet long and weighed untold hundreds of pounds. After four hours with the business end of the posthole digger, and several neighbors' jokes about reaching China, Dad had permanently located the hoop at the edge of the driveway, where by my estimation it was anchored in roughly thirty gallons of Portland cement.

As was typical, my father would relive the concrete-pouring exploits of the day each evening at dinner. The night after the installation of the basketball pole, as the family slouched around the table, he broke our food-chewing silence by stating, "I'll tell you one thing, that pole isn't going anyplace."

"No shit, Sherlock," I mumbled, as my mother shot a glare at me over the Tater Tot casserole.

More than twenty years later, and ten or more years since my parents had moved away, I drove by the low blue house last year, on the weekend of my twenty-year high school class reunion. The place is now yellow, and while the basketball hoop is gone, it came as no surprise to me that the pole remains.

While we might all benefit from some form of counseling in these times of self-improvement, I'd pay money to have some insight into the background of my dad and this concrete thing. Maybe some psychiatrist would tell Dad that he builds things because he is an only child and he's trying to build siblings, or some psychoanalyst might tell him that during that time in his life he was searching for more permanence or more order, or that he was "nesting," or had stability issues. Or it could simply be that some guy behind the counter at a hardware store once told Dad that if he wanted whatever it was he was building that particular weekend to stay where he built it, he ought to pour some cement around it. As Sigmund Freud reportedly once said, "Sometimes a cigar is just a cigar."

Looking back, I now feel I can attribute at least some of my deep appreciation for the outdoors to my dad's weekend concrete projects. Especially on fall weekends, I went duck hunting and made sure I was always out the door in the predawn, before the foreman's whistle blew. At the Larsen house, male children simply did not want to be home on a Saturday, since they would be conscripted into participating in whatever the construction project of the day happened to be. Over the years, this included breaking up sections of sidewalk with a sledgehammer, mixing gallons and gallons of water and sand and cement with a snub-nosed metal shovel in a shallow metal tub, and hauling the broken chunks of the old cement cellar floor up from the cellar one small, hopelessly heavy bucket at a time.

Many was the autumn afternoon when I'd arrive home from a morning's duck hunting, still adrenaline charged from a morning of shooting, but bone tired after rising in the middle of the night and the stiffening ride home. After emptying water, muck, and stray cattails from the boat and truck, I'd usually slink down our wooden stairs to hang whatever ducks I had in the cool basement. At about the time I had sized up the couch for an afternoon nap, the concrete foreman would stop me in my tracks to enlist my services. My dad was supportive of duck shooting and fishing, but if there were strong backs around, he had something for them to get under, regardless of what sport those backs had enjoyed earlier in the day or what time the alarm clock had gone off. My adolescent sporting career often felt more like a work release program than the carefree days afield I prefer to remember.

During and after my college years, I went on to work as a guide and wasn't home much, so I'm sure I missed a lot of construction. He never said it, but I think Dad was suspicious of the guiding profession, since hunting and fishing guides don't buy, sell, or produce anything. But I will say that after I got a pretty fair gig related to the outdoors, he has been consistently supportive. We both live in Pennsylvania now, and see each other often at the holidays and for family functions—and Dad often supervises my own fix-up projects when I'm forced to attempt some sort of home repair.

It dawned on me about a year or so ago that through all of the hunting and fishing of my youth and in twenty-some years of waterfowl hunting in my adult life, I had never been duck hunting with my father. I am really embarrassed about that fact, since for years I have sought to try and explain to him how vital the outdoors has always been to me. Oh, I thought about taking him, but never did. I took him down to the pond I hunted years and years ago one time. I wanted to deliver my decoys to the boat landing the night before shooting that particular spot. It was almost dark, and since there were no birds in the air, I doubt it made much of an impression on him. I'm sure he just saw reeds and brown water.

Plans to hunt with my father were one of those things I just never got around to. There were always duck hunting friends, other places to try, and while I got close to taking him once or twice, I was afraid it wouldn't be any good. I wanted him to see and shoot ducks. For me, it was important that he got on and rode the whole ride. Otherwise, he would never understand that while duck hunting offers none of the features of permanence that concrete affords, it can be a joyous way to spend a weekend. I have a very productive lease now and I wanted to show it to him. I'm pretty good at getting ducks into my decoys most days, and at the very least I've been doing this for a good number of years now. In my mind, we were overdue. It was time.

Which is how Dad and I have come to find ourselves in my large steel tank blind, half-sunken into a marsh levee in

Ohio, where we look over 200 hundred acres of marsh. Two hundred mallard, wigeon, and gadwall decoys tug at their short lines in front of us, bobbing in a southwest breeze. The 8:40 A.M. Conrail train, her blue engines pulling automobile carriers, coal hoppers, and flatbeds stacked with lumber, had squeaked with sounds of metal on metal and passed on the tracks in the distance some twenty minutes ago. Lake Erie is just beyond the tracks and our vision; the lake smells like the sea, and seagulls wheel high in the air at regular intervals.

Earlier, after I had waded the decoys out, we stood in the dark and enjoyed coffee in the blind. We ate cold Danish rolls from the package and watched the steam billow from our metal cups. The sun rose and filled the entire sky with the same hot orange color as the burner of an electric range. Spirals of mist rose from the water of the marsh. A little flight of wood ducks crossed the decoy spread after dawn, and while the sun now warms our backs, our gun barrels are cold. Since the wood ducks, no other ducks have worked within a cannon shot of our tank here on the levee. I stand and lean against the front wall of the blind and rest my hands in my elbows, my eyes sweeping the skies. The blind shifts a little as I lean my weight against the front wall. I am saddened that we'll likely see nothing else this morning. I just wanted my dad to have a shot at some decoying ducks. But the outlook grows grim. I was afraid of this.

Dad appears content, however, as he sits in the blind in the brown camouflage parka and cap I had issued him earlier, with his legs crossed and my over-under resting against the steel wall of the blind in front of him. He has his hands in his lap and he worries his wedding ring, spinning it slowly around his finger with the thumb and forefinger of his right hand. It is odd to see him here, dressed in camouflage. He does not look out of place, but when I look at him I feel the same surprise I have felt in unexpectedly bumping into a friend from home on a crowded street in a foreign city. Dad's face is obviously familiar, but my mind cannot frame it in this setting. As the morning passes, we have talked about football, the kids, and what kind of mileage he thinks we got on the drive over, and I'm content to kill another half hour just enjoying small talk and his company before picking up the decoys and packing it in.

Scores and scores of blackbirds weave by, and the sun is warming things up to the stage where I am trying to remove my canvas jacket. I stand there with one arm tucked under the suspenders of my waders, and I see colored reflections flash on the water before I see the actual ducks. Six mallards pass over the blind in an organized knot, no more than thirty yards high and going straight away. The last two ducks in the group had their wings set briefly over the decoys, but they keep pace with the group. I whisper sharply, "Don't move."

Dad pulls his chin into his chest and bows his head a little, and as I blow a six-note comeback call, the flock wheels over the downwind edge of the marsh and starts back. I tell Dad to get ready, and he uncrosses his legs and lays the shotgun across his lap. Still standing, I press myself against the tank blind and mix feeding chuckles with drawn-out quacks. There are two greenheads in the group, with a hen out front and three hens behind. I cannot seem to get the ducks to swing upwind to the spread, but after a minute of calling and a wide arc that takes them out over open water and back behind the blind, they are closing on the hole in the decoy spread I have left for them. Before I have to tell Dad to get ready, he has scooted himself a little farther forward on the blind's bench.

As the first hen in the group pumps her wings and glides in to land, I turn quickly to look at Dad and, in the most even voice I can muster, say, "Go ahead and shoot one."

I didn't want to rush him by sounding too hyper, and I hoped that by following my advice to shoot one, he would focus on a bird instead of making the classic mistake of the inexperienced duck shooter—zipping off two shots quickly at the group.

I note that he looks down to locate the safety of the over-under, but thumbs it off as he brings the gun barrels over the front edge of the blind. He points and swings, and as my ears register the noise of the blast, a mallard drake cartwheels in the air. The whole blind slips forward just a little, but it is enough to make me lean back on my heels to counter the movement. As the blind moves, Dad stumbles imperceptibly, but it affects him enough that he lifts his gun, holding it to his chest, barrels in the air.

35

The duck splashes crazily down and disappears completely for just an instant, then bobs up—orange feet first, breast in the air. Ripples from the splash spread and dissipate through the decoys.

"Great job, Dad! You got one, and a drake at that," I say as I work my arm out from under my suspenders, where it has been stuck through the entire episode.

"I could have gotten two, but the blind wiggled and it spooked me a little, so I didn't shoot again," he replies.

Dad opens his gun and lays it across his lap, and I sigh as we both sit down on the bench and are quiet for a minute or maybe two. I rise and state that I will go and retrieve his bird. As I pass through the door of the steel blind and ease into the water, Dad looks over the side of the blind, as if to inspect it, and says, "You know, if you poured a couple of cement footings for this tank thing, it would firm it right up."

Laughing out loud, I pick up the handsome fall drake, and as I turn to show it to him, Dad pushes his cap back on his head and I keep laughing as I watch the familiar smirk grow across his face.

F. W. Benson '31

CROSS CREEK FARMS
Quality Hay Products

02	SEPTEMBER					02
Sun	Mon	Tue	Wed	Thu	Fri	Sat
1	2	3	4	5	6	7
8	9	10	11	12	13	14
15	16	17	18	19	20	21
22	23	24	25	26	27	28
29	30					

RATACZAK '02

Chapter Four

147

I did it today. I actually succumbed to taking the calendar off the wall and counting the days until the duck season. One hundred and forty-seven days until the season opener, not including teal season. I try never to include teal season, as it is usually a disappointing day or two of swatting mosquitoes in a duck blind the temperature of a Turkish bath, while trying to hit impossible ducks with a gun that hasn't seen natural light in months. I try to forget about teal season. If the weather is cool, it is a bonus and I get to duck hunt early. It is a little game I play, the teaser of teal season. In the meantime, I keep my vigil for the real opener, with real weather and the prospect of decoying and shooting big ducks.

I feel like a kid, counting days. I'm a little embarrassed about it. I remember being eleven or twelve and doing all the day counting we did at that age. We counted eleven days until school let out, a week until the pool opened, three days until Halloween, seven more days until Christmas, or eight days until the baseball game or the

state fair. It seemed like we were always in between, counting to the next big event.

When I was in my teens, I counted the days until duck
season, but usually the counting didn't start until we were a
good month or so before the opener. Teenage day counting
usually coincided with the return to school, and hours and
hours of time to daydream about duck hunting. I remember
those years fondly. The night or two before duck season, I'd lie
in bed, staring at the ceiling, just trying to pass the time until
opening morning, but scared to death fall asleep for fear I'd
miss it. Instead I'd run through lists in my head to see if I had
forgotten anything. Finally, I would give up on trying to sleep
at all, and would start the day two or three hours early, only
to end up high-centered by the lack of a breakfast restaurant
open at 3 A.M. Didn't they know it was duck opener?

But I'm an adult now. I shouldn't be counting days until
the ducks fly, and certainly not this far in advance. I guess
if you are going to count days in the first place, it doesn't
matter where you start—although it doesn't seem very
mature to count at all. But I can't help myself. I'm bored,
and I'm anxious.

In my analysis of the problem, I've discovered that for the
first time in a long time I'm truly prepared for the duck season this very minute, smack in the middle of summer. If a
sudden cold front were predicted, or a puddle duck population explosion had prompted a special, federally mandated,
emergency early duck season to be written into law tomor-

row, I could be ready to go just as soon as I could get a pot of coffee brewed and poured into a thermos. This has never happened to me before. I usually have a lot of loose ends, new leases, lost decoys to replace, duck calls I can't find—just odds and ends to clean up. Not this year. It really isn't like me to get so far ahead of my duck hunting preparation. Frankly, if I knew I would have to suffer in this day-counting purgatory, I would have dragged my feet and not been so damned efficient in the first place.

Since the close of the last duck season, just after the New Year's holiday, and in an effort to be prepared for the season anew, I have:

1. Purchased three dozen brand-new diving duck decoys;
2. Painted over the unsatisfactory factory paint on three dozen brand-new diving duck decoys;
3. Put swivels, lines, and anchors on three dozen diving duck decoys;
4. Lost a lease on a diver lake;
5. Taken swivels, lines, and anchors off three dozen brand-new diving duck decoys;
6. Sold three dozen brand-new diving duck decoys over the Internet at a slight loss;
7. Bought two dozen brand-new puddle duck decoys with funds from diving duck decoy transaction;
8. Painted over the unsatisfactory factory paint and artistically enhanced important duck attracting

parts of two dozen brand-new puddle duck decoys;

9. Installed weights and lines on two dozen brand-new puddle duck decoys;

10. Packed two dozen brand-new puddle duck decoys into decoy bag for storage in garage;

11. Removed six dozen used puddle duck decoys from decoy bags in garage;

12. Checked lines and anchors on used puddle duck decoys;

13. Painted important duck-attracting parts on six-dozen used puddle duck decoys;

14. Emptied all new and used puddle duck decoys out of decoy bags in the garage;

15. Painted camouflage patterns on four mesh decoy bags;

16. Put all new and used puddle duck decoys back in camouflage bags;

17. Painted camouflage patterns on thermos bottle;

18. Painted camouflage patterns on coffee cup;

19. Painted camouflage patterns on flashlight;

20. Painted camouflage patterns on boat oars, boat seats, and outboard motor cover;

21. Painted camouflage pattern on portable dog kennel, figuring what the hell, I had the paint out;

22. Repaired broken zipper on camouflage hunting coat;

23. Repaired bottom of camouflage hunting bag;

24. Purchased new camouflage cap;

25. Mowed the lawn nine times in new camouflage cap;
26. Sorted shotgun shells by shot size and placed them in newly repaired camouflage hunting bag;
27. Removed perfectly serviceable camouflage tape from shotgun;
28. Replaced perfectly serviceable camouflage tape on shotgun with slightly different patterned camouflage tape;
29. Stored camouflage waders in big plastic storage box marked "camouflage waders" with permanent marking pen;
30. Removed all new and used puddle duck decoys from camouflage bags in the garage;
31. Written my name on bottom of all new and used puddle duck decoys in permanent marking pen;
32. Put all new and used puddle duck decoys back in camouflage bags in the garage;
33. Read two old duck hunting books;
34. Read one new duck hunting book;
35. Read, reread, and passively memorized eleven back issues of *Ducks Unlimited* magazine;
36. Read and marked with little yellow sticky notes important duck-attracting items in three different catalogs;
37. Removed multiple yellow sticky notes from three catalogues, citing issues of affordability;
38. Ordered plastic great blue heron confidence decoy marked

by yellow sticky note from one of three catalogues;

39. Blown hail call each Tuesday morning at three mallards sitting on roadside pond while driving eight-year-old daughter to school for early choir practice;

40. Heard "Dad, quit it, will you?" from eight-year-old daughter while blowing hail call at three mallards sitting on roadside pond en route to school each Tuesday morning before early choir practice.

It is not like I don't have a full-time job. I'm not standing in line for government cheese or collecting empty bottles to feed the family. I am gainfully employed and work all day like the next guy. All this preparation I take care of at night or on the weekend. Usually, I sneak in an hour or two of futzing with duck hunting paraphernalia after we make the kids' lunches for the next day, search behind the couch cushions for change to feed the parking meter, sign permission slips for field trips, trim the hedges, watch a Little League game, or go to one meeting or another. But when you reach a stage where you are fanatical enough to make time in your schedule almost every day for duck hunting preparation, then you don't have to reach much further to get to a place where you start to obsess about counting days.

Some noted travel philosopher once spouted that to truly enjoy travel, you had to learn to enjoy the getting there, or the in-between times, and that if you learned to do that, then you could learn to enjoy the in-between times in life. Obviously, he is not someone with any concept of duck hunting's almost addictive attraction, or someone who has read Nash Buckingham so many times he is qualified to teach a graduate course on the hunting at Beaver Dam.

Sure, I enjoy fishing, and I love to see my kids run the bases at a Little League game. Those are fine examples of enjoying the in-between times. Summer should be like living inside a Norman Rockwell painting, with swimming holes, Frisbee, fireworks, and white-painted fences. But you can only appreciate an ice-cream cone dripping in your hand for so long. In my book, it doesn't compare with a gray day in the marsh when the cattail tops are swaying and I have my collar turned up and my cap pulled tightly down on my head.

A flight of mallards is about to make its third low pass over the blind. A hen in the flock chatters back at my feeding call. I freeze stiff, stop calling, and hold my breath for a moment, though I won't remember doing it until later. Rolling my eyes up to look from under the bill of my cap, I see big green heads with necks craning to look down at decoys swimming in the wind. There is no doubt that they are going to decoy after this pass: they are flying level and have set their wings to coast more than once. This bunch just needs one more swing to get the wind angle right. At the moment the flock is over me, I hear the *wheesh, wheesh, wheesh* of the air pushing through eight or nine sets of wings, and the hairs on my neck stand on end. Under layers of polypropylene, fleece, and Cordura, I feel my arms tingle as they go to gooseflesh, and in an instant the tingle runs up my arms and into the small of my back and to my neck like a chill. I shake off one mitten, and as it hits the damp floor of the blind, the orange feet are out and ducks are backpedaling. I slip off the safety and rise in one practiced motion.

That is why I count days on the calendar. And that is why tomorrow I'll cross off another day and count down to 146. In the meantime, the great blue heron decoy is on back order, so that gives me something to look forward to.

Chapter Five

ALPHABET LOADS

Hunting snow geese may seem very plain to those who live near the gulf coast of Texas, and for those of you who do, skip ahead—since this may be what waterfowling is to you—but don't take it for granted, even if it is old hat. For those of you who have not been to the land of big country, big-haired women, and big hats, you really ought to try a rag hunt at least once or twice. Snow goose hunting in Texas has all the elements waterfowlers everywhere are looking for—open country and lots of land, little competition, big decoy spreads, and a chance to see the absolute spectacle of the wintering grounds.

Several years back, I had bothered three shooting friends about making a Texas trip to the point where I believe they finally caved in and agreed to go along just so they wouldn't have to hear my carping about it any longer. I was so crazy to see a white goose hunt in Texas—a rag spread hunt—that I think they believed I would stay and homestead if I ever got there. I recalled old episodes of ABC's *American Sportsman* television program—Grits Gresham, Bing Crosby, and Phil Harris lying in the rice stubble and chatting happily between flights of geese. I offered up little color brochures from outfitters showing big bags of snows, blues, and specks. "That could be you in this picture," I said. After what seemed like an eternity of planning, saving, and packing, we finally packed up and shipped out.

Arriving in Houston, my partners and I eventually located our small mountain of luggage on the carousel, stuffed everything into a rented van, and pointed the whole rig southwest. Unlike other cities, which gradually give way to suburbs and little mall developments before becoming rural America, Houston just stops. There is no warning. One minute, you are traveling down a busy expressway, jockeying for position and changing lanes with commuters and soccer moms on cell phones, and the next thing you know, there's a flattened armadillo in the road, a rusty Ford F150 in the next lane, and No Hunting painted on a truck tire hanging from a fence post. Here and there, lonely little oil wells nod slowly on the horizon, and their bobbing reminds me of the glass birds we had as kids that nodded and drank from glasses of colored water.

The goose hunting country begins after you pass through Wharton, and most of the guides, outfitters, and hunting clubs are centered out of El Campo and Eagle Lake, both rice, oil, and high school football towns that anxiously await the cackles and barks of the snow and blue geese that

arrive by Thanksgiving or so each year. You've no doubt seen
advertisements for one or another of these clubs in the hunting magazines; there are a number of them, and virtually all
taking paying hunting clients on a guided basis. While you
should check references, almost all of these outfits are reputable, as it takes excellent contacts and big money to main-
tain the rice field leases and the resting and roosting ponds
that hold, and put clients into, birds. Many clubs supplement
the goose season with deer hunts and quail properties, and
clubs that are not run as efficient hunting operations are
quickly washed out.

Our outfitter, Pat, met us at a gas station in town right on
time, and we followed in our van to our hunting headquarters, which consisted of two modular trailers of the type that
are the headquarters at a construction site. The trailers were
parked near an old farmstead home, which served as our bar,
kitchen, and dining facility. It wasn't anything fancy, and the
points the judges deducted for style were quickly awarded
back for an isolated location—near the goose flights, in a
peaceful setting that we had all to ourselves.

That evening—surrounded by some old decoys, victims
of bad taxidermy, secondhand furnishings, and a couple
sleeping dogs—we made ready, signed off on licenses and
Texas stamps, and, on instruction, dug into a large cardboard
box stuffed with white jackets that we were told we could
borrow for our stay. If you aren't familiar with rag spread
hunting, you need to know that there are no blinds involved.

Guides and hunters alike lie in fields among the decoys and wear white lab coats or parkas to blend in with the hundreds of decoys in the spread. Many of the jackets had names scrawled on them, either over the left breast or across the back. These white coats all appeared to be outfitters' hand-me-downs, and most were ripped and rimmed in dried mud. I picked the biggest coat I could find, hoping to accommodate my ample bulk and a layer of clothes. By chance, the jacket I pulled from the box had the name Bubba written across the chest in black permanent marker in the location uniforms normally have names embroidered on them. I swear I am not making this up. It is too corny, too perfect—too Texas to be true. Needless to say, I caught a nickname from my shooting friends faster than a four-year-old catches a cold at day care.

We also met Kenny, our guide, who, when not guiding, is a plumber of great renown, as well as a volunteer fireman. As much as military medals pinned to the chest tell those in the armed services immediately whom they are dealing with, the stack of goose bands hanging from the lanyards of Kenny's calls spoke volumes of his time in the goose fields. He had some jewelry. And if that wasn't enough, Kenny's Lab, Betsy, appeared to be from excellent breeding and carried herself with the demeanor of a Norwegian farmer's wife. She was all business. Betsy had seen hard work and was ready for more.

The next morning came fast, and we were awakened by a knock on the door in the wee hours. Stumbling from our sleeping trailers to the breakfast table, we were surprised at how warm and humid the weather had remained, even in the middle of the night. Being of the school that requires good duck weather to be icy, cold, sleeting, or downright dangerous, this was a radical change. I admonished myself for packing too many clothes. We left for the hunt in the black of the predawn wearing little more than long-sleeved shirts or windbreakers, light rain pants, white gimme caps Pat gave us for booking the hunt, and knee-high boots. We had the windows down, and as we rolled down the gravel side roads and through the rural night we left a trail of cheap cigar smoke and country radio in our wake.

On entering the rice field with your guide, the fun begins. If you have never been in a cut rice field, they come in several varieties, ranging from damp to gooey to just plain unnavigable. This one was mushy and slick from recent rains. Gray rice field mud sticks to rubber boots, shell bags, dogs, and decoys, and makes the going tough, so it is best just to be patient and not hurry the process. Kenny settled on a spot, and in about three minutes he traced a large heart-shaped area by walking along and placing white rag decoys on sticks every fifteen feet or so as he went. He did not slop or seem clumsy as he went about his work, and you got the feeling—even in the dark—that Kenny had learned much about the economy of motion in mud. He had done this plenty. Once he had finished his outline, which was perhaps 300 to 400 yards long and about as wide, he turned our group loose to fill in the spread with loose rags and rags on sticks. We stuck the sticks in the ground, waving the decoys through the air first to fluff them up. Then we draped the rags over the rice stubble. There were five of us, and this process took about forty-five minutes or so. In that time, we got about 800 decoys on the ground, covering an area roughly the size of a supermarket parking lot. Coming from duck or goose hunting backgrounds where a dozen decoys is often adequate, and 100 decoys is a lot, I felt a sense of accomplishment in just getting that kind of decoy power to work at our disposal.

With the white rags spread everywhere, Kenny pointed us to a spot near an upper atrium of the heart-shaped spread. We settled in a depression formed by the huge tires from the harvesting machinery that had worked these fields earlier, and covered up decoy bags and shell boxes and made ready. The sky was clear, and when the stars gradually flickered out as the sun begin to ease over the horizon, I could make out machine sheds, grain elevators, and the blinking lights of a water tower in the distance. Some ducks chattered as they traded over us, and a flock of cranes passed by, looking for all the world like flying stepladders—huge wings cutting the humid air and long legs trailing behind. Collectively, we sweated under our white lab coats, following the exertion of placing the spread, and I wiped a crust of mud off the barrel of my goose call.

Having hunted geese in the past, I had seen impressive flights of geese in the Dakotas and on the mudflats of

Hudson Bay, but nothing in my hunting experience had prepared me for the flight of geese I saw in the sky that morning. It started on the horizon, and as the sun rose pink and diffused in a lightly clouded sky, I saw what looked like billowing smoke from a brush fire. The birds were still too distant to be heard. Soon, white geese covered the horizon from edge to edge, and—viewed en mass—they began to cover us like a white, waving blanket. The sheer number of birds was so large, and they covered so much area, that I had the sense more of an approaching storm front than of a movement of waterfowl. As the first of the flocks grew closer, you could tell that all of the geese were well up in the sky, maybe traveling 150 yards high, but the sheer density of birds, and the barking and honking of thousands and thousands of geese, was chilling, raising the hairs on my neck as I lay watching. At times, when the flocks and waves of geese converged over us, their sounds were so loud that you could not be heard—talking in a normal voice—by the man lying just four feet away.

However, it takes rare weather and low clouds or fog to pull these large flocks, and our shooting that day was for juvenile snow geese, the gray singles that came after the huge flights had passed, and for specklebellies and small Canadas, which decoyed readily to the white spread. Kenny flew kites, with rags on the string, and as the warm wind perked up just after sunrise, these added another dimension to the layout. We lay in the mud, pleading on our calls, and though many birds would set wings and glide toward the decoys, with thousands of eyes on the ground, the snows seem possessed by what was almost a group hysteria.

We did have one flock of maybe 500 birds come to us that first morning. The leaders were a mix of snow and blue geese, with one "eagle head"—a mature blue with a white head and neck—leading the way. The flock set their wings from perhaps 200 yards high, and swirled toward the decoys in what became a white tornado, with other flocks of tens and fives and twenties joining at the back of the swirl. By the time Kenny had pronounced it time to "get 'em boys," there were geese stratified through the air in a seemingly endless whirl above us—from those about to land in the decoys, some of them just feet away, to others with wings set, still joining the flock 200 yards distant. This is rare, and produces the only easy shooting you'll often have. When it was over, we had nine snows and blues on the ground in close proximity, and Betsy was sent to clean up a sailing snow, which she did rapidly and without fanfare. It was our crowning moment for the morning, as overall, this being our first day in very new surroundings, we had all shot like tourists, especially the guy in Bubba's coat.

It takes one extremely bold bird at the front of the flock to lead a group of these geese down to the decoys. Even then, decoys usually only bring them so far, so that much of the shooting can be at fringe yardage. This part of Texas is no place for delicate duck guns, and certainly not for a family heirloom. You won't find any engraving here either, unless you count notches carved in the stock with a pocketknife. Goose guns for rag spreads are clunky when viewed as a group: big 12-gauge pumps wrapped in camouflage tape, composite stocks, 10-gauge doubles, or pumps with longish barrels and the bluing long gone. Most of these guns would blend in better if hung in the garage near the posthole digger rather than in a glass-fronted gun case in the den, and if you go to Texas, make sure you take a gun that will get the job done.

From these workmanlike pumps, autos, and doubles, only alphabet loads get the job done. Big 3- and 3½-inch bismuth or tungsten loads, or steel shot in BB, BBB, or T complete the equation. Shooting anything smaller on heavily feathered and high-flying geese makes little sense, and leaves you feeling like David trying to slay the high, white Goliath. Like it or not, you also have to get comfortable taking shots at passing geese that are forty-five yards away or better, and you have to do this while half sitting in the mud. Prepare to get used to the idea that you have to pull out in front of these birds by the length of a railroad car or so before touching off your big 10- or 12-bore Roman candle.

Goose hunts in Texas are a morning affair, and many outfitters allow geese to rest unmolested each afternoon, which helps keep them in the area. After morning shoots, we were responsible for helping with the decoys, and tagging birds and dropping them off at the picking house. We spent most afternoons napping, lounging on lawn furniture, or cleaning our guns and begging the hours to pass until the next morning hunt.

Each evening, our camp cook, Lloyd—a huge, bearded fancier of Harley-Davidson motorcycles—defied all biker stereotypes by donning a white apron and preparing tasty country food, Texas barbecue, and other local specialties. You've not seen it all until you've picnicked outdoors under a cool January sky, with chicken-fried steaks, cold beers, and distant flocks of geese trading through the gathering pink of the evening. We usually followed dinner with a fire, some more beers, and maybe some cards. But by a respectable hour each evening, everyone had watched the weather, had pissed off the redwood deck for the last time, and was snoring in his bunk.

The very best goose hunting that Texas offers can only be had in a fog, and we were lucky enough to experience this just once, on the last morning we were to be in this flat gulf country, where humid air and warm temperatures can sometimes combine to bless the goose hunter with the great equalizer. Fog is rare, but it pulls the great flocks of trading geese down from the usually lofty altitudes of their morning flight paths, and makes a rag spread seem as effective as stuffed birds. Fog shrouds everything in a gray film of sky and water, and makes these group-oriented birds—so often on the edge of the mass psychosis that keeps them high in the sky—humbled, less cautious creatures that creep across the sky, anxious to find a safe harbor for the morning feed.

We were in another rice field, a huge one this time; we knew this from scouting the previous afternoon, although now we could not see twenty yards in any direction. The field was wet from overnight rain, and rice stubble and gray mud formed huge, snowshoe-like disks around our boots, which we dragged or tried to scuff off as we walked through the field in the dark, carrying guns and laden with decoy bags. We spread the decoys, but confined the layout to a smaller area than usual, despite the immensity of the field. We kept the decoys closer together, with the hope of achieving the maximum white-on-black contrast—figuring they might show up better through the greasy clouds and air. After the decoys were set, we positioned ourselves in a ragged line, then lay down to drink RC Cola and wait.

The sun never really rose that morning; inky darkness just turned to hazy gray. Shooting time came and went, and we fidgeted on the ground, lying on our backs with nothing to see outside of a fifty-yard perimeter. At times you could see twenty yards up, and for ten minutes at a time the sky would close down to within ten feet of the ground. Sometime after eight o'clock, we could hear the first barking of snow geese and began calling in earnest. The sounds of hundreds of calling and barking white geese could be heard—but not seen— above us, but from the volume of the calling, the geese were down close. The first birds that burst through the fog arrived as a surprise. They just materialized as if by magic. One second, there was just gray haze; the next, there were a dozen bright white geese hanging in space. Kenny called the shot, and for the first time that morning, guns barked, geese folded, and all the elements came together.

The morning continued like that for more than two of the greatest hours of my waterfowling career, and we lined our bag of geese, breasts up, near us along a small dike, so we could keep an accurate count as we approached legal limits. We took turns shooting geese that appeared out of the fog— hanging over the spread as if they were standing still in the heavy air. We took photographs of the bag, the dog's retrieves, and our surroundings. We laughed and enjoyed the depth and grit and details of the experience as you can enjoy it on a morning that you know you'll remember forever—freezing instants in time like they were recorded on celluloid.

I had seen watercolor paintings of mornings such as these, and had often placed myself in them—in a hooded white jacket—smeared in mud, picturing which bird of an imaginary double I'd take first. It had been a watercolor morning, and as so rarely happens on any trip, it was the last morning before the long trip home. This always adds deli-cious irony to the packing and traveling process. I'm not talk-ing about irony in the sense that you have gotten what you came for, or "filled out"; the experience, good or bad, should always be richer than merely one of a cooler filled with goose meat. I'm talking about the irony in the heightening of your feelings—as if someone has colorized your own mental movies, but in returning to the real world you must give up the Technicolor and wait again in your world of black and white until a return to Texas, or somewhere else that you have seen in a painting or a small brochure. I'll miss wearing

Bubba's white coat. Pat made me give it back when it was time to leave. But had Bubba been with us, I'd like to think he just might have been proud. At the very least, he would have had a few laughs too.

Chapter Six

MOTION DECOYS

Whatever happened to throwing rocks? That used to be the way I did it. Ducks would work my decoys on a flat day, and my hunting partners and I would hit the calls. Then, as the birds would travel away from us, we'd lob some plum-sized rocks from inside the blind. By the time the flock had turned toward us again, there'd be plenty of wave action. Usually this was enough to turn the trick in calm weather and we got our share of the shooting. I know my premise is sound. Trading ducks like to see movement.

Several years ago, on a trip to Alaska, I had the chance to fly over the wild areas of the Bristol Bay region with an experienced floatplane pilot. It was one of the most amazing flights I have ever taken, and I still remember cruising over pine stands and feeling the lift of air as the little plane topped the ridges. I still recall the throb of the plane's engine and the sight of rivers snaking through valleys as they opened below. We saw brown bears running across the tundra, as well as a few caribou. The pilot saw several moose on small ponds that dotted the valley floors, but for the life of me I could not see a moose. Later in the flight, we flew over a large pond of perhaps several hundred acres, where water had seeped from the mouth of a small river onto a broad tundra flat. The pilot said, "There's another moose with a calf." Though I strained and pressed my nose to the glass, I still couldn't see them. He then told me that the key was to look for the movement or the ripples in the water, and follow the ripples back to see the moose. What a revelation. I began to see the animals as if they were standing on lighted platforms, waving colored pennants. It dawned on me then that this may be exactly what ducks need to see too.

I assume that man has been fooling with decoy motion since the dawn of time, hasn't he? *Homo habilis* and his neighbors in the next caves down the street crouched behind clumps of large-leafed plants, hunted over woven straw decoys, or shaped clay and clumps of mud, and would wait until migrating pterodactyls made their final swing. Then they'd launch a few rocks into the tar pit, and as the flying lizards decoyed to the bubbles and the waves, those primitive hunters would throw their spears. Later, they'd take the slain game home in a rock-wheeled cart. Of course, there was no rubber-fingered duck plucker then, or paraffin, so primitive man skinned most of his flying lizards.

Roll the clock forward a few millennia. Just two and three years ago, I was still throwing rocks. But a friend of mine named Art, who hunted with his cousins on a marsh over on the next section of land, had a jerk-cord arrangement, and they got the ducks on calm days. Our gang had spirited and competitive relations with Art's bunch. The comedians who shared my blind wittily called Art "the jerk" on those days when he outmaneuvered us with his clothesline-and-bungee-cord wave maker, but there was no denying that we had a slower-than-usual season competing with the jerk string gang in nice weather. I tried to one-up Art at one point that year with a sturdy sunken arrangement I had fabricated one evening in the garage when I should have been helping the kids with their homework. It featured the blade of a broken oar fastened inside a huge coiled truck spring, which was set upright into a five-gallon pail filled with concrete. I got a double hernia trying to move the pail from my garage into the boat, but I finally sank the whole rig in the water in front of our blind, right in the tenderloin of the decoy spread. Then I ran a stout cord back to a corner post.

On a day that was calm and warm, only a few teal and wood ducks traded about in a sky half filled with light clouds and jet trails. Mostly the ducks flew the routes they had flown all summer, and very few took the time to decoy. They had friends of their own and didn't need my plastic ones. Frankly, it was the kind of weather you'd expect for dove shooting, and my thoughts soon turned to the prospects of that, or crappie fishing. But about midmorning, I had the chance to work my new motion rig, as several mallards traded across the far edge of the marsh, interested but distant. I drew back on the cord and was briefly reminded of my elementary school field day tug-of-war, with our little feet backpedaling on the grass and our little hands clinging to a huge manila rope. After loading the spring, I snapped the cord free, and as it shot forward it shook the entire blind—scattering shotgun shells, Little Debbie cakes, and coffee cups everywhere.

I had motion in the decoys all right. The oar blade and spring arrangement produced a wave of the type seen in Japanese monster movies. Godzilla was kicking his feet in Tokyo Bay. The five decoys near the epicenter of the rig flipped straight away, and most of the rest surfed for at least a moment or two, bucking up and down like those airbrushed Mexican hot rods designed to rock up and down on their springs. Seeing the now roiling surface of the lake, and apparently sensing that a storm was brewing, the mallards just kept flying. Not too long after that, there was shooting from Art's blind. I went back to the drawing board.

Since that time, I have tried all manner of motion rigs, flippers, floppers, paddlers, swimmers, swingers, and even goose decoys with little torpedo-shaped motors. I have not tried the magic decoys with the spinning wings yet, but reports are very favorable, despite the fact that I feel they promote a more Mardi Gras atmosphere in the spread than I generally like. A friend reported that he ordered one of these whirling decoys and it worked so well that as the postman delivered the box, a flock of pintails circled the house as he came up the sidewalk. I've taken a wait-and-see attitude, and assume that magic, spinning-wing decoys will be like pocket calculators: they'll still do the math, but the price will come down or the ducks will tire of them. My focus remains on moving the water.

Some of my rigs have worked and some, like the oar in the bucket, were complete failures. I had a couple of rigs that showed promise, but the string and tubing arrangements were so complicated that little duck boats had trouble going around them without channel buoys to guide the way, and dogs often got hung up on cables during retrieves. A friend's Lab swam back to the blind one day with a drake wigeon in his mouth and enough string looped between his toes that it looked like he could make a cat's cradle with any of the kids on the school bus. At least I was getting some satisfaction from doing the rigging myself.

I spotted a great idea just last season in one of the myriad hunting magazines I have lying around the house, and I scrounged enough parts to put the thing into practice. This rig was essentially the business end of a couple of trolling motors that were bolted to a fence post, which was then staked into the bottom among the decoys. The propellers ride just under the surface, facing the general direction of the sky. Power was provided by waterproof cables that ran to a car battery in the blind, and I anchored a dozen decoys near the propellers so they would appear to be happy, bubbling feeders when I got the juice flowing from the battery.

This thing worked like a charm, pushing a steady stream of little waves all through a good-sized decoy spread. I was thrilled, and knew I could compete with the jerk-cord boys on a mint julep day in August if I had to. Although it was a pain in the neck to cart the battery back and forth from blind to boat to truck for recharging every day, it was a small price to pay. I was secure in the fact that I'd have an attractive spread even on windless days. In short, I was back in the game.

I'd hunted several weekends over the propeller rig, when one morning, in the middle of a pretty decent flight, the wind puffed up a little. Puddle ducks of several varieties had been attracted to the spread, and I had three big ducks in the bag already. Then I got greedy. Rather than pulling the cables off the car battery when the wind started to do the work for me—

relying on Mother Nature to provide the action I needed—I let things go. I reasoned that if a little motion was good, a little more was better. I mean, if you were walking down Main Street and saw a cluster of people just standing on the sidewalk, along with another group all dancing the hula, which group are you likely to investigate? Even if you have errands to run, you have to know what the dancing is all about.

The wind puffed a little more, and the weedless propellers continued to be weedless. But they proved not to be completely benign. The machine cut the first decoy cord that blew into it, and sent a plastic mallard adrift. Then, in a matter of seconds, the motor had eaten several more, as a freshening wind pushed more decoys into the path of the whirling blades and I unwrapped a chicken sandwich. When a decoy with a heavy nylon cord finally got wrapped in the workings of the propeller, I heard a hollow clunk, and in the instant I looked up from the sandwich I saw what looked like the kind of savage alligator attack you see on the Discovery channel. There was commotion in the water, and I saw a decoy being pulled under backwards. It would pop up again, only to be pulled helplessly under again and again by the spinning propellers in a froth of water and foam. By the time it occurred to me to disconnect the power, it was over. A plume of acrid, black smoke emanated from the scene of the disaster, and I got just a whiff of a smell you'd recognize if a plastic bowl ever melted across the heating element of your dishwasher during the dry cycle.

As it happened, a trio of pintails flew high over the marsh about this time. As a tip for future hunts: You can smoke in your boat or your blind, but smoke in the decoys puts trading ducks on the defensive. The pintails went over to Art and the rest of the jerks, and I heard the sound of shotguns, followed by dog whistles, in the distance shortly thereafter.

Since the trolling motor episode, I have stayed away from anything electrical, and while I long to find the perfect solution, I draw my personal line at hiring divers to do underwater welding for me. Divers are listed just after ditch diggers in the yellow pages, but it just isn't in the hunting budget. I have focused my attention on little battery-powered quiver wigglers, the hockey-puck-shaped disk you can get from the catalogs or even from toy stores. These little battery-powered disks vibrate forcefully enough that they move the decoys around in the calm, and pose little fire risk. However, for the amount of batteries I'm burning up, I could send that pink bunny that advertises batteries off to play his drum on another coast, so I'm reconsidering the diving idea.

As a frisky aside, the little quiver pucks are fun in the off-season. In addition to being a duck hunter, Art is also one of our church ushers, and he is often my target for a senseless practical joke. I caught his eye in church the other Sunday, and as he passed the collection basket I dropped a quiver puck in among the folded bills. As I squeezed his arm, I whispered with some conviction, "Feel the power from on high, brother Arthur."

Art had a pretty good sweat on his brow as he collected the tithes from those seated in the back pews, and I had a chuckle as he steadied the arm carrying the basket by clamping his free hand over his wrist, as if he were taking his own pulse. The reverend appeared happy, and he smiled broadly as Art strode purposefully back up the center aisle. He assumed Art was supporting the weight of the burgeoning collection basket. Meanwhile, my wife had put two and two together, and I got an elbow in the ribs along with the suggestion that had any of our kids pulled that stunt, "We'd be getting postcards from the reform school about now."

Art was chagrined, but he was laughing by the time we reached the coffee and doughnuts in the church basement. We had a fine talk about the duck season, water levels, and forecasts. I didn't bother to tell him that I had started underwater welding classes over at the vo-tech school. He'll see the fruits of those labors next duck season.

Chapter Seven

THE PHONE CALL

O n an evening exactly ten days before Christmas, my wife and I finished putting up the family tree. It was a nice Douglas fir that was a little too tall for the room, so I had sawed some inches off the trunk. I argued valiantly for locating the tree in the dining room, but was overruled. In hindsight, if there is one fight in your marriage that you will have annually and never win, it is the discussion on where in your home to place the Christmas tree. This is a battle all married men must lose. Take your lumps and put it where she wants it. However, you must know that this will be a particularly difficult battle to lose, because you'll already be aggravated by having tried to get the tree upright in the flimsy metal stand in the first place. I cranked down those little thumbscrews, or eyebolts, or whatever hardware the Taiwanese manufacturers of Christmas tree stands include in the tree stand kit, then cranked them some more. After the third try, with an inch of pine needles blanketing the floor of the porch, I dragged the tree inside. It stood erect, and I headed for the garage to tackle other projects.

I was putting up shelving. While there were still sixteen days left in the duck season, I had been frozen out for two weeks. Ice and a blanket of snow ensured that all of the ducks and even the last of the geese were gone. I had moved the car and truck out, and had brought all of my decoys, gas tanks, bags, and hunting paraphernalia into the garage. I was in the process of screwing shelves into the walls, so that I could store hunting gear in a more orderly fashion. Perched on a ladder, I was surrounded by a pile of hip boots, waders, camouflage knee boots, and plastic storage boxes, which covered the floor. I had mislaid the cordless screwdriver, and was retracing my steps through the garage trying to locate it, which proved to be like searching for the Northwest Passage. I looked in drawers, in nooks and crannies, and on shelves I had put up just an hour earlier. As it is with all things lost, the harder and longer I looked, the harder I felt I had to look to find the damned thing and the more frantic I got.

Then I got the phone call. For my entire adult duck hunting life, I had been waiting for the call. I had read about other hunters who were lucky enough to get it, and friends had told me about it, but I had never gotten one. This is not the call from one of your hunting friends who wants to try out this spot or that on Saturday. It is the call from someone in the know—a camp manager, a farmer, or a friend at the destination—saying, "The ducks are in, and the time to come is now." Nash Buckingham's best duck stories tell of riding the train to his father's duck camp after receiving the word, or the message, or the call. Sixty-odd years ago, Gordon MacQuarrie wrote about getting the call from a man I presume to be a resort owner in northern Wisconsin. I fondly recall reading and rereading the stories of how he and "Mr. President" would pack a big American car and drive through wind and dark and snow to get to their cabin, usually pushing snow with the front bumper of the big car for the last several miles to get there. When MacQuarrie finally arrived, the resort owner already had the generator on and the fireplace stoked, and in one or two stories, all involved would gather after dinner at the edge of a Wisconsin lake to hear the sounds of thousands of ducks stirring in the darkness. There were pats on the back and handshakes all around for having hit the flight ducks just right. I had dreamed of having that happen to me for years, and had often felt that a situation of that kind would be the culmination of years spent chasing ducks, but I never had anyone call me. I hunted by myself or with friends—hunting when I had the time to go and taking my chances.

But here I was, sifting through shoes and boots and boxes, and more boots. I was disappointed that my duck hunting was over and done for the year, and the stress and shopping and decorating for the holidays weighed heavily on me. And then the call came. My jovial friend Ed related the news that he had just received his call from Rocky, the manager of a private camp on a small island in Canada. Rocky had said that even though most things were frozen solid, currents around the island, which sat near the edge of Lake St. Clair, had kept three or four spots open, and there were a lot of mallards and black ducks around. One of the camp's members had left after a fast-limit shoot that afternoon. Ed cautioned that, while he had total faith in Rocky's report, the weather was marginal and the ducks could pack their bags any minute. The plan called for quick action: I should depart first thing in the morning, in order for me to drive three hours to Ed's house, then ride another three hours with Ed and his friendly friend Dave over the border into Canada, so we'd have a chance to get in an afternoon shoot. Ed added that even though the camp had twenty or so members, Rocky had tried to contact many of them and nobody was able to make it on short notice. We'd shoot an afternoon, and then overnight at the camp and try a hunt the following morning before we departed.

My frantic search for the cordless screwdriver ended abruptly, and I sat on the pile of boots and decoys and other hunting debris as Ed explained the details to me. I was so excited, I heard only snippets of his explanation: private duck club; we'd be the only duck hunters there; blacks and mallards; open water; winter weather; a reliable report that there were a lot of ducks; and Ed and Dave, who together have hunted ducks enough for three lifetimes. My brain churned. Tomorrow was a workday and, to make this trip, I would have to call in sick. I hadn't bought the first present for anyone in the family for Christmas. In addition to being at the boiling point of duck hunting tolerance for the duck season that was effectively over, my wife was coming down with a cold. My daughter had practice for the village Christmas pageant, my son had a doctor's appointment, I had debris of all kinds spread far and wide across the garage floor, and I'd never get the vehicles back in the garage tonight. The right thing to do was to stay home and get things taken care of, but this was the phone call. I'd never had the phone call before, and who knew if I'd ever get one again? I told Ed I'd be on the road at five A.M., sharp, and then I practiced my sickly voice for the call to the office.

Twenty hours, 367 miles, one unpleasant border crossing guard, and several laughs later, I was shown to my simple but cozy room in the camp. Across a narrow hall from the room that Ed and Dave shared, I struggled to get my bulging duffel bag onto the bed. I had hurriedly packed far too many clothes, plus waders, caps, mittens, and boots. As I pulled my knee boots out of the bag, a cordless screwdriver dropped onto the wooden floor with a clunk. I smirked. Clearly, it had fallen off the ladder and into a boot last night. Ed cast his shadow across the door frame and said, "I see you expected our camp to be in some state of disrepair!"

I stammered on about putting up shelving, and the ladder, but Ed was having none of it. He was already joking with Dave about a guest who brings his own power tools, and

Dave chimed in that the door to their room was a little sticky, adding, "While we have some soup, you could work on the door if you also happen to travel with your own planer." Their comments were in good fun, but I was embarrassed nevertheless.

At lunch I met Rocky, a tall and extremely affable American Indian with bright eyes, a sly wit, and a ponytail to his waist. He had settled into his chair at the head of the long table, and among the waterfowl prints and worn varnish of well-used camp furniture Rocky summarized the season and migration for Ed, Dave, and me. Not knowing any of the locations, areas, or numbered blinds he talked about, I was fascinated to hear about the limits from the Long Pond, the Round Pond, or Mutt's Point, and a day—early in the season—when the teal had come through. I had the sense that Rocky was one of those rare people who has been in the center of a prolific duck area all his life, but has still not lost any of the wonder or fascination that ducks and duck hunting hold, and doesn't take any of it for granted. He told a story about a clear, crisp October afternoon, when he said the sky was pure blue and there was hardly a cloud in it. Ringbills had shown up in little flocks, and Rocky expected a big push of these calendar ducks soon.

Rocky continued, "That evening, about the time the sun was thinking about setting, the ringers started to come. You couldn't see them—they were flying so, so high—but you would hear them come. I was in the kitchen when I heard the first bunch, and I went outside to look. I couldn't see a duck in the air, but I heard this sound, and the next thing I knew, there were hundreds and hundreds of ducks pitching into the marsh. They made a noise that was hard to describe, falling from so high so fast that they sounded like a marble rattling down a pipe. By nightfall, there were thousands and thousands of ringbills here."

But that had happened almost two months ago, and the ringbills were long gone. The comfortable little camp on the island was surrounded by ice; a foot of snow blanketed the ground and lay in loaves on top of the doghouses. Out the front window, not quite a mile away on the ice, was a line of ducks that appeared as a ragged black string in the distance. Rocky suggested that we set up shop in a makeshift blind nearby, and that those ducks, mostly mallards, would work their way to us as the afternoon went on. After lunch, we bundled up and very carefully picked our way through the ice and slush in one of the camp's aluminum skiffs. It was a gray day with a warming wind from the south, and while a steady procession of swans migrated by, very few ducks checked in with us. Mostly the ducks just sat far, far out on the ice. Near dark, we pulled the decoys and motored back to the little cluster of low brown buildings with white trim, and the warmth of the camp. As we motored closer, the smells of wood smoke and baking mingled with the cold air currents.

That evening we enjoyed a simple meal of roast beef, potatoes, and gravy, followed by a berry pie served to us by a petite American Indian woman named Wanda. She'd slip into the room with a slight smile, and then disappear as fast as she'd come in. After dinner, as the logs burned down in the camp fireplace, Ed and Dave said their good nights, but too wound up to sleep, I shuffled about our camp building quietly, looking at the maps and photos and prints that clung to the paneled walls. The camp was not big—just a half dozen bedrooms with a couple of baths in the halls, plus a living area, dining room, and kitchen. Under a covered porch were a row of plywood lockers filled with waders and camo parkas and hats. Throughout the camp, the furniture was not too new or pretentious to be comfortable, nor too old to be serviceable. When you sat in a chair, you knew for certain yours wasn't the first butt to fall into it, but you also knew the stuff wasn't so dilapidated you were afraid you'd catch something. Out the window and across a small canal, light shone off the black covers of six identical outboards, which hung from six identical camouflage boats, each piled high with decoys. The overall effect of being in this place was not unlike wearing a favorite pair of slippers. Everything here had purpose and authenticity. There were no frills, no pretenses, and no silly extras. This was the compilation of every duck camp I had ever read about. Eventually, I cracked the window in my small bedroom, and as I slipped off I heard the faint quacking of contented mallards on the cool night wind.

As I blinked awake in the predawn, I heard the wind first. Even as I turned on the lights and came fully awake as my bare feet hit the cold floor, the moaning of the wind vibrated the very walls of the small camp, and bitter cold air seeped through a crack at the bottom of the door. The comfortable little enclave that had felt like a small castle surrounded by canals seemed to take on a more defensive posture as the cluster of small buildings huddled against the wind. Outside, a bare bulb that lit the path to a small boathouse swung rhythmically on its wire, and the thermometer on the covered porch read 12 degrees.

We were left to our own devices for breakfast, but Dave had eggs and sausage well under way in the camp kitchen by the time I had a cup of coffee in hand and offered to help run the toaster. Ed and Dave are both serious duck hunters—as serious as they come—and even in this weather, the question of whether we'd go out this morning was not raised. We were headed out to try and get some of those late-season ducks close over the decoys. We had plenty of clothes and parkas along, and Ed joked that his only real late-season strategy is to stick his calls inside his coat to keep them warm, rather than letting them dangle on the lanyard on the outside of his jacket.

As a winter sun tried, ever so slowly, to crawl over the horizon, the snow cover added to the available light. We beached the eighteen-foot boat on the edge of the ice surrounding a snow-covered, round island of just an acre or so, and slid over ice-coated gunwales into shallow water. Small slabs of ice cracked off and floated free as we waded ashore. The leeward side of the island offered only a small space of open water, not much bigger in size than a public swimming pool. While Dave stowed the boat and covered it with decoy bags, white sheets, and some branches, Ed and I waded out three or four dozen decoys, and then we frosted the cake by placing a dozen full-bodied mallard decoys on the ice near the open water. The floating decoys stood out well on the hammered-metal surface of the water, and the decoys on the ice were even more visible. We cobbled together a blind with more white sheets and branches, and sat on a root-tangled ledge of the mud bank, under two tall trees that were the only thing more than three feet tall across the entire horizon. The rest of the world was gray and white for miles in any direction. A hen mallard tried to land in the decoys before we got our guns out of their cases, and I took her early arrival as an omen that we were going to do well.

We sat for a long while, and in the cold distance we heard swans barking. Not long after that we saw a small flock of Canada geese race downwind, flying low and straight and looking for shelter. There were small knots of diving ducks in the air, but the big puddle ducks were slow to move. I was clapping my leather mittens together to stay warm when Ed reached over and laid his gloved hand on my arm. With his other hand, he gave a short highball, and a flock of seven big ducks worked upwind over the ice and toward the spread. Ed gave a three-note landing call, while Dave and I gave feeding chuckles softly. As the ducks reached that imaginary point in space where you expect them to lock wings and glide to the decoys, the flock moved in unison and climbed away from our water hole, scaling the two lonely trees. A hen quacked in alarm, and our pleading calls would not bring them back. Two more groups of ducks came to us in the next several minutes, with the same reaction. We had things about 98 percent right, but could not get these late-season mallards to commit to filling in the last little piece of the puzzle.

"They won't finish because of the trees," Dave surmised, and Ed agreed it was either the trees or the boat. Dave took offense, since the boat was hidden perfectly, and from fifty yards away you could hardly tell there was a boat there. "Oh, don't get your hackles up, Dave," Ed said. "I'm not saying you didn't hide the boat; it is just a big bump—but it is a bump that wasn't here yesterday." I offered to wade the boat out and anchor it away from the island, and did so, while Ed and Dave shifted the bulk of the decoys as far away from the trees as they could place them in the open water. As I waded back to the island, a drake mallard sailed in from the gray sky and pumped his wings several times before landing on the edge of the ice with the decoys. We stood out in the open, and watched him look over the situation and begin to preen. Things were looking up.

"Two o'clock, pintails" Ed whispered, and by the time I looked out from under the brim of my hat, five slender ducks were over the decoys. "Get 'em," Dave barked, and I heard the audible click of Dave's safety coming off as I pressed my own. I pulled in front of a perfect drake pintail, his breast whiter than the snow itself, and he shuttered, then crumpled at my shot. Dave had collected two drakes from the back of the group. I waded out to pick up the birds—anxious to see what I knew would be heavily feathered late-season ducks—and heard Dave question Ed behind me, "Why didn't you shoot?"

"I thought I would save the last of those ducks for someone else," Ed replied.

"Save them for someone else?" Dave said. "Did anybody save you any buffalo? No, they didn't. Get in the game. This could be over in minutes, and you know as well as I do that this will almost surely be the last hunt for a long time."

Dave has about three serious bones in his body, and from the tone of his admonishing, I knew we had things clicking now. Between them, Ed and Dave had hunted nothing but ducks for a total of eighty-five years, mostly together. Dave wasn't really chastising Ed. It was more a private partners' code that said, " We're into them now." Meanwhile, it seemed to me it was going to be a rare day.

And rare it was. The next two shotgun shells fired from my banged-up old autoloader killed a red-legged black duck and a greenhead that was decked out in all his winter finery. Ed and Dave had killed three or four birds apiece from each of the following flocks, while I handled the calling details and looked on. The realization that I had killed the perfect trio of what I considered to be the most desirable of all the big ducks while shooting 100 percent had me giddy. I laid the threesome side by side in the snow, and admired the contrast between the long lines of white and chestnut of the bull sprig, the dusky brown of the black duck, and the greenhead's gray tuxedo. I was as content as I could possibly be.

We watched a flock of six or seven mallards circle a wet spot on the ice a half mile or so away. After seven or eight swings, they finally set down, and even from a distance I could tell they were standing on the ice. Several minutes later a single joined them, then a pair, and then three more mallards bypassed us to land with the building group far out on the lonely ice.

As five more mallards flew high over our spread, Ed said, "Watch this!" and I prepared to hear him blow one of his long highball calls to try to turn the ducks back, something I knew would not happen. Ducks decoy to live ducks, period. Instead, Ed waited, and as the flock set wings to land a half mile away, Ed blew a three-note landing call as the mallards flared and then set down.

"Did you see how I landed those birds?" Ed asked, with a twinkle in his eye. He added, "A lot of guys can call ducks and land them in a decoy spread, but there aren't a lot of people who can call and control ducks at long range like that. Setting those ducks down at long range is like making a 300-yard shot with a good rifle—it takes years of practice."

Dave allowed as how Ed would have plenty of time to practice now, as those live birds were sucking every duck in the frozen country into them, and unless we shot or disturbed them we were through for the day.

Thankfully, the next ducks that tried to decoy were single mallards that arrived only a minute or so apart, and on the same flight path. Both worked snappily to the call, and came to us before they saw the building group on the ice. Ed and Dave killed a drake each, and at the report of Ed's Beretta the distant group left for quieter climes. Dave's shot on his greenhead was particularly impressive. Dave is not just a good shot; he's a great one. He has about perfected shooting a falling duck that he suspects is crippled in the air, if it shows any signs of life at all. This is a tough shot, if you have never made it. Imagine standing at sidewalk level and trying to hit a falling grapefruit dropped from the third floor. It is pure Isaac Newton.

I was content to let them have the shooting, as I was half afraid to shoot at another duck for fear I'd miss and break my streak. Just one of the dumb numbers games I get caught playing with myself—the most or the fewest—or whatever. Still, I had climbed my personal little duck hunting Kilimanjaro, and I didn't want to come down.

By midmorning the wind had begun to carry sleet to us, and our hoods went up at about the same time as the sleet began to hammer us horizontally. At times the sleet would change into small beads of ice for a few seconds, which made it feel like it was raining machine screws. But for the most part, sleet came as blobs the consistency of baby food, slung through the air as if thrown from the spoon of a very strong child. It dawned on me that except for the colors of the ducks we'd bagged, a painter could have captured the entire scene with nothing but a wash of white and blue, along with gray and brown; the beauty of the day was in the urgency of the season and its simplicity. The ducks quit flying as the weight of the sleet increased, and we scanned the skies from under our hoods, broke out a thermos, and waited.

Dave whispered to me that, any second, Ed would be launching his winged pilgrims speech—something he does, Dave explained, when the shooting slows. Not three minutes later, and to nobody in particular, Ed began: "Behold these winged pilgrims, denizens of the north, sliding southward on strong, swift wings. Gaze in awe at their grace as they travel invisible corridors across the northern skies. We as flightless mortals remain powerless to join them on their journey, which began thousands and thousands of years ago, and will continue long after we are gone. We encounter these intrepid travelers only briefly along their way, though our very souls would have us wish that we could join them."

I was speechless. I couldn't think of a thing to say in reply, nor did I know if a reply was even appropriate. Dave meanwhile told Ed that he liked it this time, particularly the part about the flightless mortals.

"I just added that for today," Ed responded, "I thought it put us nicely in the scheme of things."

I got the impression this was just another of the games these partners played—a goofy dissertation that had turned into a tradition after it had been repeated over many days spent killing time while scanning empty skies. The sleet pelted us, and a big, single black duck tried to sneak silently, wings cupped, into the decoys. Ed rose up quickly and, in one movement, peeled his hood back with one hand and raised his gun with the other. Ed hit the black hard with the first shot from his Beretta, the report of the shotgun making a strange sound as it ricocheted off the ice. The second shot folded the duck for keeps, and it splashed among the decoys.

"You almost didn't get the job done with that winged denizen," quipped Dave.

"Very funny," replied Ed. "You should remember Montaigne, who said, 'I quote others only the better to express myself.'"

To which Dave replied that Ed might remember the quote of Dorothy Parker, who when challenged to complete a sentence with the word horticulture in it, stated "You can bring a whore to culture, but you can't make her think."

While the situation was sublime, it seemed that the conversation had moved to the ridiculous. As we were full up on black ducks and only two mallards shy of being limited already, Dave suggested that in light of the quality of the sleet, we might think about picking up before it started to freeze on the roads toward nightfall, which would make our way home treacherous. So, all kidding and quoting completed, we slid wet guns into wet gun sleeves, and quickly lined up sixteen big ducks—drake pintails, blacks, and drake mallards—on the boat seat and took a quick photograph for posterity. We then tightened up our hoods and cuffs, picked up the decoys, and motored back to the small lodge.

Packing our belongings, we said good-bye to Rocky and, after transferring to a small boat and then to a bigger boat, we were soon back in Ed's Suburban for the trip home. Ed and Dave sat in front. While I tried to be a good guest and fight sleep, the rhythm of the wipers scraping the sleet and rain off the windshield soon had me dozing across the back seat. When I awoke, we were almost to Ed's house, where I'd pick up my truck to continue my trip home.

"Did you get cold back there?" Dave asked.

I replied that I had been very comfortable.

"We had to open the windows so the noise of passing trucks would drown out your snoring," Ed joked.

As we pulled into the driveway, Ed chuckled and I rubbed sleep from my eyes and tried to regain my composure. We moved my luggage from Ed's truck to mine, and after dividing up our birds, we stood under the cave of Dave's garage to get out of what was now just hard rain. Dave's duffel bag sat in the driveway while he looked at some loose plastic on the running board of the truck parked in his driveway. Ed told him to get out of the rain—he needed to say good-bye and get headed on home. I was anxious to get going too, and still had three hours of driving to do. I couldn't understand Dave's sudden fixation with his truck.

"Just one second, Ed," Dave said. "I think I could get this fixed easily enough. Does anyone have a cordless screwdriver?"

I never saw it coming. After some handshakes and pats on the back, I waved out the open window of my truck as I pulled out of the driveway. I chuckled to myself as I settled in for the drive home, and started to give some serious thought to doing my Christmas shopping.

EAT YOUR VEGETABLES

My wife is a vegetarian.

She is young and fit, and it would not surprise you to learn this if you met her. She is the type. She quit eating meat at fourteen or fifteen, I think because it was the thing to do. She is not, however, one of those who lecture others on the evils of meat, or killing, or farming or ranching. Not eating red meat was just her deal. It was a conscious decision on her part, but it was made at a time when girls make lifestyle decisions they often keep throughout their adult lives: to eat or not eat meat, to pierce their ears, or to get a tattoo.

When I met my wife, some years ago, I was a casual meat eater, and when we started dating I found myself not eating meat in her company, just because I thought it might offend her. I quit eating meat altogether. I woke up one day and realized I had not had a steak or a hamburger in three weeks. So I pretty well stopped eating red meat, really as a contest with myself. I wanted to see how long I'd last. I didn't miss it much, and it didn't take a whole lot of discipline on my part to just take the steak out of my evening meal, or skip the big double cheeseburger at the drive-through. I spent a lot of time in Argentina some years back, and ate more than my share of "cut it with a fork" steaks in those days anyway. It may sound spoiled, but there were not a lot of steaks here at home that impressed me all that much. I ate fish instead.

Besides, there was the hormone concern, the antibiotics concern, mad cow disease in Europe, *E. coli*, and everything else you have read about in the news or heard about near the watercooler in the office. Chickens don't look much like chickens anymore; most of them never leave a square cage just big enough to house them, and many of them are forced to gobble more steroids than a lot of television wrestlers, at least on a pound-for-pound basis.

But as a hunter, I faced a moral dilemma: the moral obligation that calls upon me, and all of us, to complete the circle and consume the game we so actively pursue. I had always eaten shot game, and while I gave some deer meat away to friends or coworkers or neighbors, I just could not bring myself to part with ducks. The connection with ducks that you have killed while calling them over decoys is almost spiritual. You can even call eating your birds an opportunity to return to a much more basic time in man's development on this planet, but that is something none of us contemplate much—to complete the circle of harvesting game.

I know I don't think about it much. I'm more concerned about the action when it happens: the calling, the decoys, wind direction. I'm trying to make the shot, or trying to get a double. I'm trying to avoid shooting the birds I know my partners are looking to shoot. I'm looking for drakes, and am often concerned about conservation issues and numbers in the heat of the action. Once the dog hits the water, there are congratulations in the blind, the pause to admire a great retrieve, the reliving of the moment the birds turned, and slaps on the back for the caller who turned the birds in the first place, or for the caller who coaxed them back.

Or my focus often changes to legal obligation and the rules levied by the hunting lawmakers. These are laws I must comply with or face stern personal consequences. The counting begins: four dead on the water from that last flock, two already in the blind from earlier this morning, no hens, one canvasback, three more, only one pintail, or seven more to fill out. Daily limits are not like a construction contractor's bid for a job. You can't just get close and still miss a little on the high side.

There is so much going on in these scenarios that many of us fail to reflect on the gravity of hunting. Erich Fromm once said, "In the act of hunting, a man becomes, however briefly, a part of nature again. He returns to the natural state..." I'm often so happy, or proud, or—on a slow, bluebird day—flat out relieved to have killed a duck over my decoys, or a specific duck—maybe a big greenhead or sprig—that I fail to reflect that the bird lying on the wooden bench in my blind was perhaps on the northern side of the Canadian border last night.

I had a duck dinner this week. I grilled breasts from several mallards I took earlier in the week on a bright, crisp day that put brightly colored, late-season ducks over my decoys. This simple dinner was a time for reflection, and it was magnified by the fact that I eat so little meat in the first place. I felt it was truly an event. But it wasn't a fancy dinner, no silver or crystal, and there were no guests. Therefore there was no boasting about the freshness of the game or posing about bringing home the fallen to add to the family larder. We are living in a land and time of excess, when most of my neighbors stalk the supermarket aisles for their meat and vegetables, so there should be no room for boasting by anyone, as surely hunting is the least effective and economical way of gathering food. For most of us, gathering any type of food we wish is as simple as a short drive to the grocery, where watermelon and tomatoes are always in season, kiwi fruit looks like something that might be interesting to try, and meat comes hermetically sealed on little foam trays, accompanied by a little maxipad placed beneath it in order to soak up any unsavory fluids.

I must make the time to consider more deeply the gravity of what hunting is, the blood sport that consumes so many of us. It goes beyond admiring the plumage of an adult bird, or remarking on the plenitude of a species during a specific time of the year.

In Europe, at the end of driven shooting days, fallen game is saluted. First comes the display of often a hundred or more birds presented in an orderly fashion, usually by lining pairs of birds on the ground. Further, sprigs of pine are often placed in the beaks or bills of game birds, as a symbol of renewal and new life. Hunting horns often play a specific salute, and in Scandinavian countries a clergyman sometimes recites a prayer. This is certainly formal by the standards of those of us who hunt for pleasure, but shouldn't we strive to adopt an attitude that at least leans in that direction? Especially so in these times when guns and hunters and hunting are being attacked on all sides. By understanding what it is we do, we reflect more fully upon ourselves—who we are and the choices we make. Whether we eat meat or not, how we treat our friends, the goals we have for ourselves, whether we will let our children see a specific movie, whether we'll have a few drinks and still drive home. The way we value hunting is part of the influence on our own standards and can act as a metaphor for our complete lives. The country club set have long suggested that you can get to know someone better in four hours on the golf course than by spending a month with him in the office. This is a pleasant, but perhaps left-handed way of saying that you can easily find out if someone may cheat. I believe this applies to the duck blind as well. Perhaps not in the concrete way of watching whether people follow the rules or not, but certainly in the grace they display as they consider the gravity of their actions.

In hunting we choose to react, and in moments we initiate life-and-death decisions. We may spare some lives for as trivial a reason as the birds may be a little too high. Or we pass on hens because we are told it is a good idea to do so. While I will not place pine sprigs in the bills of my harvested birds, or feel compelled to say a eulogy, by cleaning and eating my birds they become part of me, and I complete my own small and special circle. I continue to respect my wife's decisions, although I hope she will some day understand the depth of mine.

Chapter Nine

A FAMILY PLOT

"Looks like we're in for nasty weather."
—Credence Clearwater Revival

I had been watching the weather reports closely for a few days, and something pretty big was happening. A November storm front added to its own intensity as it climbed over the Rockies, after leaving the West Coast drenched. Meanwhile, a huge pressure ridge sagged south from Canada, and red and blue bars hung across the television weather maps like electronic barbed wire. The weathermen seemed confused, or at least nobody seemed willing to show all their cards. Even better, different weathermen offered vastly different reports. One of the television suits thought it would miss us, but the radio said to prepare for colder weather. I have always believed the radio guys. Somehow the fact that you don't see them, and can't critique their nightly outfits, lends credibility to their opinions.

A day later the Dakotas were locked in cold and wind chills dipped below zero. Temperatures had plummeted, and the national news showed Dakotan ditches littered with cars and trucks up to the door handles in snow. Small airports closed. When one of the local weather pundits stood in front of his glowing national map and used the magic words "Alberta Clipper," I assembled gear, put hot water in the thermos for the night, and packed the truck. This was winter cold. Outside I could feel the cold iron taste on my tongue, regardless of what these weather guys had said.

The mortal fear of missing my alarm clock left me fitful in sleep, and I spent much of the night napping in bursts, hearing the house creak and watching the clock's digital numbers change for minutes at a time. By four o'clock I had given in. I left my dark neighborhood and headed out of Minneapolis down an empty highway. My younger brother Chris was with me. Chris is a big strong kid, well over six feet, Norwegian features, and dishwater hair combed only by his fingers. He's in college, and we don't get to hunt together as much as we'd like because of the demands of school on his time, but this seemed like a good day to play hooky. "You win and organic chemistry loses. Come and get me," he'd said a day earlier.

Chris has a large, casual presence, and when he jumped into the cab of the truck, he filled it up, stretching his long limbs across the bench seat. In a giant flannel shirt, plus layers of turtlenecks and insulated underwear, he alternately balanced and sipped at his coffee, used his finger comb, and worked the dial on the radio as I tried to time the green lights as we drove through town. Chris used his sleeve to wipe the frost off his window, and if this proved to be like other drives, as I continued along he would peer out into the passing night and make a quiet, but running, commentary on points of interest as we passed them by.

The car dealership just off the cloverleaf was deserted at this hour, but it advertised low interest rates, and offered the time and temperature on a sign that towered over the lot. Vinyl pennants waved on their long lines and bounced in the light over new cars and trucks. It was 4:37 and 26 degrees. I looped west, heading out of the city. Mile by mile the malls gave way to scattered islands of light, and then the horizon grew darker. I could feel the truck pushing against a headwind, the kind you could feel and hear from inside the vehicle. I looked back into the bed of the pickup to be certain the boat was secure. The bags of decoys rode snugly between the boat seats. I had tied a big red rag to the prow of my skiff, since it hung out of the bed of the truck for at least a yard, but there was no one behind me to appreciate my thoughtful gesture.

The road narrowed to two lanes of blacktop. We rolled on through several small towns, and main streets were deserted. It was still too early for bakeries to be open, or for school buses or anyone working an early shift to be on the road. When I slowed for the two stoplights in Hutchison, it did not escape me that both of the lights were swaying on their guide wires. The clock at Twin City Federal Savings showed 5:04 and 21 degrees, alternately, in large, green digital numbers. I was reminded briefly of the hours I had just spent watching a smaller set of green numbers on my clock at home, but things were moving faster now. Judging by the stiff flag fully unfurled over the hardware store, the wind was as least thirty miles an hour, probably more. The wind chill would be well below zero, and the wind itself would be the only thing keeping water open today. Cracking the truck window confirmed the bitter wind and temperature, and I had the feeling that I was letting the warm genie out of our comfortable truck cab bottle, and quickly wound the handle to seal us up again.

A half hour later we were on gravel, and I made the turns in the dark that we had made getting to this pothole many, many times before. We didn't always have this spot to ourselves, but we usually did. Years ago I had stumbled upon this pothole, and had then discovered that it was marked incorrectly on the map. It was supposed to be a mile to the west. I never did write to tell anyone at the mapping company.

The late-night disk jockey had signed off the radio, and as we continued west the radio reception got poorer. Chris rolled the dial, looking for "duck hunting music," as he called it, but gusts of wind brought the A.M. programming to us in intermittent, scratchy waves. Then we heard a recorded rooster, and a silly song announced the start of the morning programming. It was 5:35, and the weather front was the news story. School closings were next: the schools were closed in every town we had just passed through. There was no serious snow in the forecast, but Chris had predicted that. "Too cold for snow," he had said earlier.

Stopping in a dirt pullout, I sent Chris out to unlock the gate, and he closed it behind the truck as I pulled into a picked cornfield. It was so cold I involuntarily tucked my arms against my torso as the door opened. Chris jumped back in, shaking his hands and rubbing them furiously a moment later. As he wiped away the drip from his nose, he had a look on his face that did not represent his normally casual way. Chris had a way of avoiding my eyes and looking at his lap when he was concerned about an issue with me. I had seen it time and time again when we were growing up, usually at a time when he had second-guessed me, before we got into some kind of trouble with Mom and Dad. This gesture told me that he wondered about jumping into a boat today. We had hunted together a lot of days over a lot of years. Chris is always game, but I knew this reaction, and I knew to take it seriously. But I also knew that this could be the big morning, the really big storm, the kind of day Chet Reneson spends his life painting. We were too close now just to sit in the warm cab of a truck and watch a stillborn sun die in its attempt to rise over the marsh that was just in front of us.

We bumped along in the cornfield for the half mile until we got down to the fence corner, and then we pulled up our turtlenecks, zipped on our parkas, and jumped out into the dark night. By the time we had gotten the boat unloaded and eased over the fence, the tip of my nose was raw cold and my ears felt frozen. Clearly it would take all of the clothes we had to make this morning even remotely tolerable, despite excellent odds at taking ducks that should be moving frantically after riding out last night's storm. We ducked into the warmth of the truck cab once more, and I pulled on a woolen balaclava, a pair of old-style "chopper" mittens (with wool inside and a heavy leather layer out), waders, and my heavy, rubberized parka.

"Jesus, it is really bad out there," Chris remarked, as he dressed likewise, with a woolen face mask and all of the additional layers he had with him. That done, he tied his hood beneath his chin, and I was reminded that my grandfather, who farmed the northern prairies all his life, once said that cold weather really isn't serious until you tie your hood.

We intended to hunt a prairie pothole that lay roiling in the dark before us. Though it is just a little clear-water marsh of perhaps thirty or forty acres, we heard waves lashing on the surface over the roar of the wind. This little lake is rimmed with cattails, and small islands of cattails and bog moved freely about the marsh as the wind dictated. Formed from water draining into the only large depression in the middle of several sections of farmland, the lake had been surrounded in past years by sunflowers or soybeans. This year the crop had been corn, but it had been plowed under. This morning we struggled against the wind and cold, and dragged our boat and gear over the frozen black slabs of earth left exposed by the plow. Dirt and grit that had not yet fused into clumps of frozen black earth blew into our eyes and teeth. In front of us the black water of the little lake bucked and lashed like the grandest storm at sea.

At the end of the marsh, near where we usually parked our truck, there was a small family graveyard that sat up on a gentle rise of land, and I thought about it as we dumped the decoy bags and loaded the boat in the mud and chop. I had visited the graveyard before in daylight, and often wondered about the occupants. There were just six or seven headstones in a small square plot, and all the graves faced the morning sun. More than once, sitting in my boat on bright mornings, I had seen the white granite of a headstone give off a pearl glow in the first light of day. But the plot was unkempt— overgrown and overrun by tumbleweed, tall grass, and this- tles. It was cordoned off from the marsh and from the fields that surrounded it by a rusting, white steel fence with a small gate secured by wire. In the dark, and when the crop was down, I marked my way in the marsh by steering the boat toward this square of fence that was the only feature on the near horizon. This morning it was too dark even to see the fence or the graveyard. Chris and I worked by feel. With the wind screaming in my ears, I found myself thinking about the graves. I often wondered about the cause of those settlers' deaths. Had a family been killed en masse in an Indian raid? That seemed a little melodramatic. What about fire, or flu, or smallpox? Did living family members still come to this little hill to cry or place flowers and grieve for loved ones who lie here? Had a wife cried over a lost husband, or a father over a lost son? How long had it been since someone had cried near these graves on this little hill?

Warmed to perspiring by dragging the boat to the edge of the cattails, we waded and launched into the dark water among bright green algae that clung to our boots along with the stink of rotting and mud that blossomed on the coldest of air. The wind raged about our heads and pulled at our jackets. Even though the cattails were blown almost flat, the thick vegetation above the water's surface protected the boat and made poling smooth. We soon broke into open water, and crossed the open pothole with relative ease. All of the small islands and bog had been pushed to the south end. It was easy enough to get to the northwest part of the pothole where, with the wind at our backs, we began to place our mix of decoys. By flashlight I could see the light reflect off the film of ice that formed on every surface of the boat that water and air touched. I spit on the metal seat, and then watched it freeze into a lump on the drab aluminum.

After decoys were set and a rough blind was folded from cattails, we waited out the dawn. I created a makeshift windbreak for the back of our blind with decoy bags and the extra oars. However, the little thermometer that hung from the zipper on Chris's jacket now showed 15 degrees, and I felt the wind was gusting past forty miles an hour. In the cattail blind the wind sounded like a freight train was passing. By shooting time, several decoys had already tipped in the wind, weighed down by the ice that formed on them as soon as the waves wet their surface. I huddled over a small cup of coffee as if it were the last sparks of a dying fire, and Chris poured coffee over the tips of his fingers, then pulled his gloves back on in an effort to keep his hands warm. Then in a feeble attempt at dark humor, he commented, "Jack London would have killed his dog by now."

The legal shooting time was 6:49, but with the legally appointed hour, no flight of ducks came. At 7:15, there was still no movement of birds. It was as if the howling wind and ravaging cold had blown everything on earth flat. Only a few red-winged blackbirds sulked among the cattails, but none dared to stray from what little sanctuary they had from the

cold. At full sunup, there was a ray of light on the eastern horizon, but the sun soon fizzled behind the gray bank of heavy weather, and there was no change in temperature with the dawn. We pounded our hands, and I stood up to dance on the floor of our aluminum skiff. I hoped this would keep the blood flowing in my chilling body, yet I was afraid to stand up completely, since the cooling of the wind negated the effect of the exercise.

At almost eight o'clock, a pair of bluebills came to our rig, and as I was dancing at the time, I could not get to my empty gun. Chris upended the drake with his second barrel, the shots almost soundless as the reports were whisked away on the wind. Feeling that he was sufficiently dead, we left the drake to float to the other end of the pond. A few minutes later, with gusts of wind rushing over the cattails, I missed a decoying canvasback with two shots. The flap of my hood caught my gunstock as I swung at him. At nine, we added three mallards to the bag from a flock of eight—a high point in the morning. Our shooting was just clumsy poking at ducks that hung straight downwind above our ice-coated blocks. After anchoring one greenhead that was still lively on the water, we left the mallards to float away on the waves as well.

By 9:30, our situation had become critical. Chris could not feel any of his fingers, and their numbness was starting to cause him real discomfort. The coffee was gone, and I knew one of my feet was frostbitten, or was close to it. I could tell my ears were frozen too. What had started as an exciting outing to challenge the weather and meet storm-pushed flight birds had now turned into a scary little battle with the elements. We decided that to stay any longer was foolhardy.

We tore down the blind and got the oars placed in their locks, and as I poled us to the edge of the bog, Chris waited to dig with the oars, spin us about, and keep us pointed straight into the wind. We only needed to pick up our decoys without incident and cross 400 yards of open water and waves, and then we could skid our boat into the protection of the growth of the shoreline. From there, we could walk easily to the truck, with its promise of heat.

Chris beat on the oars and held the boat steady, but green waves broke over the transom of the little boat, and more spray froze instantly on the floor and seats. Another wave and more spray, more ice. I had to yell to be heard over the churning water and wind, and my brother, just a yard away, could barely be heard as he yelled directions back. By the time I had four decoys wrapped and thrown onto the floor, ice had formed a shell over the back of the skiff. It was becoming more and more impossible to pull the decoys from the water, as they were coated with ice and many of them were half submerged. When ten decoys had been retrieved, Chris pulled us back to the cattails, where we beat the ice off of the surface of the boat with our hands and with the oars and pole. Chris's hands hurt him and I could see real pain in his eyes. I retrieved a knife from my bag, and on our next pass through the decoys I cut cords. Sacrificing cords and anchors seemed a small price to pay for the speed of throwing blocks into the skiff as fast as possible. The entire boat, along with all of its contents, was now covered in clear, hard ice and the wind raged all around us. Ducks had started to fly, and a number skated onto the far end of this little marsh, but we no longer cared. We were spooked, as our morning episode had suddenly taken on overtones of survival.

The back of Chris's coat and hood were stiff with frozen spray, and my leather mittens were frozen into twisted blocks. The boat was sitting low in the water, the weight of the ice pulling it down. We got the last of the decoys in, and set off across the opening. It was too rough for me to pole standing up, but I sat against the transom and pushed hand over hand, as Chris dug in with the oars and pulled our skiff across the pothole. When we reached the other side, Chris quickly waded out of the boat and walked, then ran, to the truck. As I collected our ducks from the base of the cattails, I could see the plume of exhaust rise from the under the truck bed, and knew warmth was close at hand. I wanted only to gather our possessions and get warm.

Minutes later, I piled into the cab of the truck and pressed my bare hands onto the warm dashboard. Chris had been there long enough that his frozen hands had started to slowly come to life, and the pain of the thawing process was excruciating for him. He could not sit still—he sat on his hands, rubbed them together, pressed them between his thighs, or held them under his arms as they tingled to warmth. It reminded me of the times when, together as kids, we had dared each other to eat ice cream fast. We'd wait for the awful moment when the mind-numbing headache locked onto our foreheads like a vise. There was nowhere to hide, and we learned that to appear tougher than the other guy we had to ride it out.

The windows were coated with frost and the humidity from our breath, and from the ice and water on our clothes. My ears burned, but I knew this was nothing like the savage pain Chris was feeling from the very meat of hands that are slowly warming, with every nerve coming to life at once, from the inside out. He would have to endure half an hour of building, lonely pain. Chris cried out and cursed, and I saw tears roll down his cheeks. I got out of the truck, and as a blast of wind slammed the door closed it drowned out his cries. In the raging wind, I paused to look out over the lonely graveyard. Turning back to see Chris's writhing outline through the frosted glass, I thought it strange that there was again crying near the graveyard on the hill. I hurried to load our gear into the bed of the truck so that we could start for home.

Chapter Ten

ARGENTINE PRIMER

I t was shaping up to be a classic morning by my aesthetic standards. I had parked my borrowed truck on a pullout of a lonely gravel road, and after shouldering my decoys, gun, and kit bag I crossed a wire fence and made off across the gummy, black mud of a cut cornfield in the dark. It was slow, sloppy going, but even in the dark I could see the faint, silver reflection of the small pothole and, as I drew closer, the small windmill nearby. Gray, scudding clouds driven by a brisk wind passed low overhead, spitting the half-rain, half-sleet television weatherman now like to call a "wintry mix."

I roughed out a small brush blind on the upwind side of the pond from sticks, camouflage netting, and tall grass that I had pulled from near the base of the windmill. After placing my decoys, I enjoyed the makeshift comfort of a dry seat— made from a stump and a short piece of board I had managed to scrounge—as I pulled my hood up and waited for daylight to arrive in this remote place, familiar in that it resembled the farm country of Nebraska, Kansas, or Oklahoma.

I had scouted this two-acre pond yesterday when I had been hunting nearby, and it had been covered in ducks that had been drawn here by about a foot of water and by not only picked corn, but cattle grazing the picked corn. This is not something to bring up at your next cocktail gathering, but ducks love to feed behind livestock that are feeding on corn. It is easier for the ducks to feed directly from cow pies than it is for them to scavenge through the field for waste grain. I don't believe further explanation is needed, for fear of drawing too vivid a picture, but suffice it to say that I had seen a lot of ducks and a lot of cows in here yesterday.

The dawn was slow in coming. The sun's light held off for almost an hour before the sky relented, allowing light to brighten the eastern sky. As the first sliver of light appeared, I heard the whistling of wings, along with the soft quacks and chatter that announced the morning flight had begun. Then three slim ducks appeared from the gray sky, and I rose to greet the lead pintail, which was now hanging suspended twenty yards above my decoys, wings set and feet outstretched. So began another July morning in central Argentina.

Pages and pages have been written on every aspect of waterfowl hunting in North America over the years, so much so that it would lead the average hunter to believe that waterfowl are virtually nonexistent on any other continent. But, in truth, there are waterfowl on all of the world's continents except for Antarctica, where you'd have to make do with penguins.

South America, and Argentina in particular, plays host to a colorful variety of waterfowl species, none of which exist in the Northern Hemisphere. Virtually all of the continent's duck, or "pato," species are actively hunted by visiting hunters from the north and by local hunters. However, a lack of waterfowl hunting tradition means that little or no decoy shooting is practiced, except by outfitters who are entertaining hunters from the United States and Canada. Virtually all ducks bagged by local hunters are taken by pass shooting near the northern marshes and rice fields of Argentina, or by pothole jumping in the central parts of the country, where corn and other cereal grains are grown, and where there is a belt of pothole country similar to that found in the Dakotas. Hunting pressure is non-existent, and in a four-month season the whole country of Argentina would have less pressure than opening weekend in a big duck hunting state such as Wisconsin.

What pressure exists is largely hunting for the pot, and many rural children who have not reached the age where they are able to use firearms hunt ducks with small boleadoras, or bolos. This is a traditional hunting tool used by native Argentines, and in larger sizes these are used to hunt the ostrich-like rhea, as well as large mammals, such as the guanaco, a beast—similar to a llama—that roams Argentina's plains regions. The bolo used for ducks is made of two lead balls, each about the size of a shooter marble and each fastened securely to opposite ends of a two-foot length of limp wire. The bolo is deployed by pinching the wire in the center, spinning it rapidly at one's side, then releasing it up into the air and into the path of passing ducks. The bolo is surprisingly effective at knocking down passing ducks at ranges of up to thirty yards. However, it must be used where ducks are passing in concentrated fashion, as well as in a dry area where the bolo can be retrieved after a hit or a miss. It would be impossible to collect your shot charge after each shot you took at a duck, but imagine if you had to collect your plastic wad each time.

Of the fifteen or sixteen species of ducks in Argentina, there are three or four standouts that every hunter should know about if he or she is even contemplating a trip to Argentina. The first is the rosy-billed pochard (*Netta peposaca*), which is locally called the *pato picazo*. As a pochard, the rosy-billed duck is genetically linked very closely to the canvasback, and in the hand the females of both species are virtually identical. The drake is a robust duck adorned in shades of black and white, much like scaup—but with a flaming red bill that features a fleshy knob just at the base. Rosybills fly like canvasback, in small groups or V-shaped larger flocks, and they decoy like the large divers as well, often angling across a marsh in compact groups or in short, straight lines. They will often wheel over the edge of a marsh or pothole before a last pass and then plunge at the decoys. Unlike the canvasback, the rosy-billed pochard is not solely a marsh duck. Instead, like the mallard, the rosy will walk about to feed on dry land in agricultural areas. Its call is the raspy *brrrrrr-brrrrr* sound associated with other diving duck species.

The pintail of Argentina is a shapely duck called the yellow-billed pintail (*Anas georgica*). Found in Africa, as well as in South America, this species is much like our sprig, flying high on trim wings, then dropping into decoys from great heights. The yellow-billed pintail whistles, and can be found in rice fields or in small shallow marshes, or often in flooded grainfields. They are a favorite of visiting hunters from North America, since they are found in shallow-water areas and can usually be decoyed in a very traditional fashion, with hunters in hip or knee boots, hunting from small brush blinds near a pothole or any shallow body of water. The perfect decoys for the yellow-billed pintail are gadwall decoys, brought from North America and modified by painting the bills rain slicker yellow.

Yellow-billed pintail are often mixed with a slightly less abundant but extremely beautiful duck, the white-cheeked pintail. This duck is also referred to as the Bahama pintail, as the Latin name is *Anas bahamensis*. The white-cheeked pintail is the court jester of South American ducks, with the brightest costume of all. Its overall color is cinnamon, but the cinnamon body features a creamy white trim package that extends from low on the throat to the base of a red bill, all edged in turquoise iridescence. Wings are blackish in hue, with a green speculum that contrasts with the red bill.

In addition to the pintail species, there are other prairie-type ducks, including the red shoveler (*Anas platalea*), the Brazilian duck, or Brazilian teal (*Anas brasiliensis*), and a handsome little teal called the silver teal (*Anas versicolor*) that will remind you of a greenwing teal. The silver has a dark cap over the top of his head, down to his eyes, with a beautiful bill of soft yellow and robin's egg blue. Named silver teal for a silvery-ash-colored hind area, the back half of this little duck looks like polished metal. Of course, like all teal, the silver is an expert at screwing anyone wielding a shotgun into the ground—or buzzing by so low and swiftly that many of us never have time before there is no time left.

Another notable duck that inhabits the land of the Southern Cross is the *pato sirir*, or *pato pampa*, more commonly known as the white-faced tree duck (*Dendrocygna viduata*). Known by many as the *cee-dee-dee*, for its whistling call, the white-faced version is a close cousin of the fulvous tree duck, which is often seen in Mexico and even in the southern United States. This is a lanky duck with big wings, and on land it stands taller than a pintail. But these ducks are mostly feathers; in hand they weigh about as much as a pigeon. They don't decoy well and are usually high fliers, easily noticed since their feet overlap their tails in flight. However, they are beautifully marked—russet colored to burnt orange through the body, with a cheek patch that looks like a Canada goose in reverse. Instead of coming down from the eye under the throat and back up, the white-faced duck's cheek patch covers the front half of the face and goes over the head, giving the effect of a duck wearing a bonnet.

There are more ducks in Argentina and elsewhere in South America, but many are rare and are not as likely to be encountered in a hunting situation. Other species include a wild, flight-capable Muscovy—enormous black, goose-like ducks that are the first cousin to virtually every farmyard duck in North America.

But Argentina is not entirely a bed of roses for the traveling hunter. As impossible as it may seem, in Argentina's northern areas, ducks are still poisoned routinely each year by rice farmers who seek to protect their crops from mass concentrations of ducks that descend on rice fields. Huge flights of ducks, mostly the prized rosy-billed pochard, pull the tender, new rice shoots from the ground each Argentine spring. Unenlightened farmers, seeking to protect their money crop, lace rice fields with poisoned corn, and ducks literally drop in their tracks. At one time I believed that these stories of thousands of ducks poisoned overnight in a rice field were purely a form of bravado from hunting outfitters, as some sort of macabre way of telling me just how many ducks they have down Argentina way. But, since that time, I have seen one of these poisoned fields, and it is absolutely the most sickening sight you could ever witness in the outdoors. Not only are ducks killed by the thousands, but collateral damage is done to everything from hawks and falcons to house cats, foxes, and farm dogs. The only effective way to stop this poisoning is to pay landowners for shooting rights, and in that way, the more visiting gunners Argentina receives, the better.

If you have the time, money, and inclination to head south some summer for a duck hunt in the South American winter, you will almost without question enjoy yourself, and you'll be likely to encounter at least five or six of the South American duck species. You'll also enjoy the chance to hunt in a friendly, democratic country where the dollar has an edge over the Argentine peso, where you can eat just about everything you see that looks appealing, and where you can drink the water without paying for it later. A quirk you are likely to encounter in Argentina, however, is the habit Argentine air passengers have of giving the flight crew a spirited round of applause after a commercial flight has landed safely. When I get on an airplane, I expect them to land it safely. For me, that has always been part of the deal.

You'll be safe both day and night both in Buenos Aires and in the countryside, and you should find it exciting to hunt in a spot where hunting tactics for decoying ducks are still just evolving. You cannot buy a decoy or a duck call anywhere in Argentina, so much of the hunting knowledge outfitters employ has come from the north, and most are eager to learn from their guests, who often show them some North American tricks of the trade.

But you might learn something from them too. I recall a trick I learned from a guide I had named Monson, a Guarani

Indian who lived in Argentina's north near the small rice-producing town of Goya. He was an interesting man who was all bone and sinew, and he reminded me of a Masai tribesman. Monson lived in an old brothel near Goya, with his wife and ten children, and he once told me the old whorehouse was a perfect place for his family, since each child had a room of his or her own. There was no bickering, either, because all of the rooms—located on either side of a central hallway—were the same size.

Monson did something that I have since incorporated into my own hunting. While sitting in a blind, he would always be certain to have a short palm frond or a piece of leafy plant with him that was large enough to cover his face. As ducks would work our decoy spread, Monson would cover his face with the frond, as a partygoer would shade his or her eyes for a masquerade. By doing this, he could look up and watch the ducks work without fear of spooking them. I have since learned that a gloved hand, with fingers spread wide open, works as well and allows you to sneak a peek at ducks that may be inbound.

If you head south to the land once ruled by the Perons, you are sure to have a fine time. You'll also be able to bring home some birds for mounting that are sure to jazz up the mantel. Imagine yourself telling your friends about the crossing shot you made on the rosy-billed pochard that is now flying across the wall of your den. Just don't be too disappointed if they leave when you start to drag out your slide projector—they're likely to do that regardless of whether you have just returned from Argentina or the drugstore. I know that is usually what my friends do to me, and that is what friends are for.

Chapter Eleven

CAMOUFLAGE

I s anyone else about ready to call it quits on the whole camouflage thing? I, for one, have finally reached my high-water mark on the eighty-seven different kinds of camo clothing I need to own to be a successful duck hunter. Not so long ago, you really had only two choices, and they were familiar. You saw the stuff in all the World War II movies, and the blotches were all the same, nondescript—blotches. There were no sticks or leaves or dimensions. Just two flavors, mostly brown or mostly green—you took your pick.

Now, there are patterns for marshes, sloughs, swamps, bays, bayous, riverbanks, ponds, creeks, and corn. There are specific patterns for springtime mushroom hunting in the marshes, midsummer in the bayou, a light dusting of snow on the swamp, and tree-stand hunting the creek with your silhouette stark against an overcast sky with light wind. Hasn't this gone too far? I have a photo on my wall of some post-depression-era hunters with strings of ducks hanging off an old, round-shouldered Buick. They are wearing plain, three-button canvas coats, and based on the number of ducks hanging off their car, they did just fine without fancy waterproof, windproof, and briarproof camouflage. I once read that in those days hunters often rubbed canvas jackets with lard to keep them waterproof. You might find a lard-rubbing Web site today, but you don't want your kids to look at it. Life was simpler then, and still they seemed to kill their share of ducks without any camo pattern. Even easier, those early-day hunters probably wore the same coat to the barn, to the shops, and to the football game.

I was flipping through a catalog the other day in search of a camouflage ball cap. I just wanted something to wear in the early season, or to keep the sun out of my eyes while I'm fishing, or to change the oil in the truck. After half an hour of perusing different options in various catalogues, I had my possibilities winnowed down to eight different camouflage patterns. I thought I could just pick out a hat and call a toll-free number, but I ended up feeling like I was trying to pick out colleges for the kids. I haven't gotten the cap yet, since it has been backordered—my bad luck for ordering at what must be the height of mushroom hunting or some such. I don't recall what I finally decided on, but I recall it being vaguely leafy. I know I ruled out any of the gray patterns. I had this premonition that gray might blend too well into the garage floor, and that it was entirely possible that my wife would run me over if she pulled into the garage while I was lying on the concrete while rewiring the trailer.

Speaking of fishing caps, while thumbing through the catalogs, I have also seen some shirts in "fishing camouflage" that sport a pattern of what looks like little horizontal blue waves printed on blousy-looking summer shirts. To me, this fishing camouflage looks like something Don Ho should have worn to a weekend of Hawaiian National Guard training. Take notice, Mr. Walleye, that shiner minnow you are now considering as a dietary supplement may not be the genuine article. It may be attached via fishing line to the guy in the little blue waves shirt. It occurs to me that, in all likelihood, the guy in the shirt is likely to be standing in a sixteen-foot boat the same color as the body of a jet airliner. The parallel in duck hunting would be to dress up in brown camouflage and build your blind out of aluminum foil. Might the boat spoil the camouflage effect of the blue wave shirt, or maybe tip the fish off? A guy has to think so.

There are not only vast selections of different kinds of camo patterns, but also some are trademarked and others are the official patterns of racing cars, conservation organizations, and parts of North America. Of course, I want to buy new hunting stuff because I like to buy new hunting stuff, but now I'm going to start feeling guilty if I don't buy the stuff that pledges my allegiance to the right racing team or endorses a conservation group. I'm the victim of the same peer pressure mentality that plagues teenagers who need to wear the "right" brand of jeans so they can fit in with their friends at the mall. At this stage, I'm afraid that if I show up at the marsh without my official or commemorative-edition camo, the gadwalls won't let me shoot at them. Most don't now, so I'm at least used to the rejection.

On a related note, last season I was setting decoys, and while I started out to set a traditional J pattern, it dawned on me after first light that my decoy set was in reality in the shape of a famous running shoe company's trademarked swoosh. I wrote them a thoughtful letter, making suggestions on camouflage, gear, and a whole line of accessory items, such as flashlights, watches, casual sportswear and après-hunt wear. I also asked for a sponsorship or an endorsement. I have not had an answer back from the shoe company yet, but I saved a copy of my letter, so if they try to do any of this without me, they can look for a lawsuit. In the meantime, I have decided to move the bluebills out of the crook of the swoosh and go back to the plain J pattern for my everyday hunting, as I don't want a trademark infringement problem of my own.

Here's a dilemma: Can I wear Mississippi River Bottom Corn Stubble in a cornfield on another river system? Will honkers on the Platte River reject me or shy from the decoy spread? Will mallards on the Ohio know immediately that I'm out of my element? I hate the thought that I might cross state lines and drive right into another camo pattern without knowing it. I read the other day that there is an up-and-coming goose and duck hunting area in Texas where the birds are attracted to peanut fields. I already have my eyes on a new parka in Fall Migration Creamy. I haven't read the fine print yet, but apparently you would only wear the Fall Migration Chunky on windy days.

+ + +

And it isn't just clothes anymore. Now all of the tools of the trade are painted or wrapped or manufactured to blend into the surroundings. Go to the gun store some day and try to buy a gun made out of metal and wood. Every duck gun I like the looks of seems to come in some sort of camouflage. I'd be scared to death I'd lay the gun down in a cornfield to go answer nature's call, and not be able to find it again until they plowed in the spring. When my hunting partner chastised me for not covering up my green metal thermos bottle during the early teal season last year, I felt the pressure to conform, and came equipped the following weekend with a camouflaged model. I had half a cup of coffee from it on opening day, and then lost it on the floor of the blind for three hours. I had to empty my partner and the dog out of the blind, and then shuffle along the floor like I was killing time in the halls of a rest home until I finally bumped into the thing.

I see now that several of the catalogs offer camouflage living room furniture. I'm of two minds with this stuff. As a rabid duck hunter, in my mind's eye I can see myself with the footrest up in a big, overstuffed, camouflaged lounger, with the business end of the clicker pointed right at the television. My wife wouldn't like it, but I believe I could watch more football if I wore the same camouflage pattern that matched the chair. I'd sit still, blend right in, and she'd likely walk right by. With luck, she'd probably miss nagging me to put up the storm windows until it was too late. But if I buy the whole camouflaged furniture set—the couch, the love seat, and the ottoman—I'm afraid she'll walk in one day, not see any of the well-camouflaged furniture, and think someone stole the whole living room.

Some of this camo stuff can be dangerous. Camouflaged baby clothes? Cute. But sit the baby down in the yard for one second to play with the dog, and unless he squirms, you could lose him altogether. Most parents wouldn't think of putting their kids in anything but special flame-retardant pajamas, but you get a duck hunter in the house, and next thing you know, every little carpet crawler in the place is wearing an old flooded timber pattern jumpsuit and blending right into the wood paneling while they color on it with crayons.

But for me, perhaps the cruelest of all of the camouflage items is the luggage. First of all, do any of us really need to travel with our hunting clothes hanging in a Marshgrass three-suiter? I thought not. On those rare and wonderful occasions that I get to travel by air to somebody's duck camp out of state, I have enough anxiety about all of my belongings getting there in the first place. I don't want to have to worry about the baggage handlers forgetting to load my duffel because it was superbly hidden in the back of the cart or mistaken for a bag of leaves on the transfer belt.

I have had a novel idea about all of this camouflage stuff, though: I have designed stationery and typing paper in the Correction Fluid and Coffee Stains pattern. I'm sending my tax return to the IRS copied on it. I figure by the time they find my paperwork on their desks, I'll have a plausible excuse for why I took a drooling Labrador as a deduction.

OUR PATRON SAINT

It must stir up all his senses
In a kind of inside grin
When he gazes down the south way and
Sees his squadrons winging in.
—Jack Herity (Belleville, Ontario)

I t was one of those pleasant August evenings that we often have in the late summer in the Midwest. I had the garage door open, and moths filtered in near the rafters to enjoy their dancing and banging around the bare bulb in the fixture on the ceiling. There was a baseball game playing from the paint-splattered hulk of a radio on the tool bench in the corner, but nobody paid much attention to it. Every now and again, a little puff of breeze would blow grass clippings up against the belly of the yellow dog lying on the concrete drive, and the grass or his dreams caused him to bat at his nose with a paw from time to time. In the distance, the sounds of neighborhood lawn mowers and kids heading home on bicycles mixed with the croaks and pings of blackbirds and grackles winging by in the gathering pink of dusk.

There was just the very faintest puff of cool in the air, and as several of us sat around my garage I could sense the first hint of excitement about the fact that fall would soon be upon us. There was little talk about team sports or the kids getting ready to head back to school, and already there seemed to be the first palpable twinkle of anticipation as we modern-day hunter-gatherers huddled in our suburban cave. In our old golf shirts and grass-stained sneakers, those of us who longed for our family crest to feature crossed pumpguns displayed on a field of marshland camouflage were preparing for crisper days that were just a calendar page flip away.

Some duck hunting friends and I were sitting on a collection of milk crates and lawn furniture for the ritual painting of bluebill decoys. Last year we painted the mallards, this year it is the divers; it has been a nice little tradition we have kept over the years. Since paying attention to the color scheme on your average diving duck decoy is about as mentally taxing as laying sod, our conversation was lively. It turned to great and poor dogs we have had, where we should move this blind or that, and ideas about trips to Alberta or Oklahoma or Kansas, or to any of the other real or imagined duck meccas we hoped to visit. There was an occasional boast about a long shot (now longer) recalled, or talk about who was fixing a gun, reloading shells, buying a boat, and the like.

But as the evening wore on, our conversation turned more philosophical. We discussed the various merits of conservation organizations, and who had done a lot for our sport through the years. Then, through the smells of cigar smoke and flat marine paint, one of the more intellectual members of our group asked who could be identified as the true father of duck hunting.

"I mean, you know, if you had to build a statue," he added.

"Good question," we all replied.

In the discussion that followed, it was noted that archery had Fred Bear and big game hunting had Robert Ruark, Ernest Hemingway, or Teddy Roosevelt, to name three. Sport fishing had A. J. McLane as the central figure in the last 100 years, and there was also Zane Grey. Fly fishers point to Izaak Walton or, for those who go way, way back, Dame Juliana Berners. Or they may also choose Lee Wulff, if they prefer to identify a more modern hero. Wulff was the Arnold Palmer of fly-fishing, bringing a hidden, and often elitist, sport to the people. Wulff also helped duck hunters in a roundabout way. It was assumed at one time that if you fell into the water wearing chest waders you would surely drown. Wulff jumped off a bridge into a river in chest waders just to prove that the waders themselves wouldn't drown you, and that the water inside the waders weighed the same as the water outside.

But as waterfowl hunting evolved from market gunning, there was no real father of the sport, as we now know it. Nash

Buckingham would be one possibility. He popularized duck hunting as sport at the last turn of the century, and his stories are filled with beautiful and vivid descriptions of genteel southern folk, twenty-five-a-day mallard limits, and the elegant duck clubs of the Old South. But Buckingham did not know diving duck hunting or sea duck hunting, and he was not well known by many who lived and hunted their ducks in the north after the war against northern aggression. Besides, Buckingham is as likely to be remembered for his noted contributions to field trials, quail dogs, or horseback quail hunting.

Perhaps George Bird Grinnell was an option? He was a focused practitioner of the wildfowling trade, and his book *American Duck Shooting* is a classic. In the humble and practical opinion of those gathered in the garage, Grinnell's book

should be required reading prior to the purchase of a duck stamp. Or Van Campen Heilner. If you have not discovered his *A Book on Duck Shooting*, I envy the pleasure you'll have in reading it for the first time. Gordon MacQuarrie? Although beloved by the group gathered in my garage, those in attendance shot down MacQuarrie's election to waterfowl sainthood as it was felt that like Buckingham, he was too geographically focused. Never mind the fact that many of us could recite lines from "The Bluebills Died at Dawn" the way summer stock actors recite lines from Macbeth. MacQuarrie was hard-wired for duck hunting, but as far as any of us knew, he had never been out of Wisconsin. A hunter from California or the Texas coast wouldn't know MacQuarrie from Machiavelli.

Joseph Knapp started Ducks Unlimited, or at least he is given credit for organizing the first meeting of the organization. It was suggested that he would be a good choice. Here was a single person to take credit for bringing the duck population out of the dry, cracked prairie of the dust bowl of the 1930s. All agreed he deserves due credit, but we lacked knowledge about him, and frankly, we needed a story. One of our crew, who insists on shooting a rusting, humpbacked shotgun that is long overdue for replacement, suggested John Browning, but he was shouted down with boos and laughter. Since this conversation was purely hypothetical, in any case, there was no correct answer, and we were having fun with this. It would also be fair to interject that since this friendly debate was taking place in my garage, adult beverages were being served. Then someone suggested Jack Miner.

If you have not heard of Jack Miner, but are an avid chaser of ducks and geese, don't feel like you have missed the last bus. There is little written about the man known as Wild Goose Jack. But Miner's legacy is a strange and wonderful story, which centers on ducks and geese and the mysteries of migration, as well as on his deep religious beliefs.

Born in Ohio in 1865, Miner was "not suited for school," and spent his youth in creeks and lakes, marsh and woods. By the late 1880s he had become a professional trapper and market hunter, supplementing his family's income with profits from shot game. But after founding one of the first game protection organizations, Miner did something that no one had done before. He bought and built his own private refuge in Ontario, the Jack Miner Bird Sanctuary.

By 1906, Miner was being called the Father of Conservation by the Minneapolis newspaper—this at a time when most folks didn't know what conservation was. Only four years later he pioneered the process of banding birds to learn about their migration habits, something else no one had done before. His first banding was truly completed in 1910, when a doctor from South Carolina returned a duck band by mail. Miner was instrumental in banding both ducks and geese through the first forty years of the twentieth century, and it was his data that was largely used to establish the Migratory Bird Treaty in North America. This seemingly simple process, which we as hunters now view as merely "collecting jewelry," began the era of restrictions on duck and goose hunting, based on the concept of renewable populations—preserving waterfowl populations into the future.

Not only was Miner a scientist, but he was one of the charter members of the Outdoor Writers Association of America in 1927. By 1929 he was honored with the Outdoor Life Gold Medal for "the greatest achievement in wildlife conservation on the continent."

Although his name may not be a household word, Miner was listed after his death by Canadian newspapers as among the "fifteen great personages of the world," an honor he shared with Shakespeare, Pasteur, Bell, Edison, Churchill, and Washington. Several U.S. newspapers placed Wild Goose Jack as the fifth-best-known man on the continent, after Ford, Edison, Lindbergh, and Rickenbacker. He had banded more than 50,000 wild ducks and 10,000 wild geese on his sanctuary in Ontario by the time he died in 1944.

Those who might be familiar with the Jack Miner Bird Sanctuary and the unique bird bands they continue to use today may know that Miner not only investigated the scientific aspects of migration, but also sought to spread knowledge of God and the Bible to those who would come into contact with his work. As early as 1915, Miner included a verse of biblical scripture on all of his bird bands, and he called these banded ducks and geese "missionaries of the air." Bird bands being as small as they have to be for live ducks to carry

141

them through their daily lives, the scriptures are short. Just a verse such as "Behold, I Come Quickly" (Rev. 22:7) is stamped into the metal above the address of the sanctuary in Kingsville, Ontario. One of the smart alecks in the garage suggested that they must have been banding teal with that one.

Regardless of the depth of your spiritual beliefs or your religious persuasion, there is no denying that anyone who has ever spent time watching a marsh come to life on the orange- and red-streaked clouds of dawn has been aware of the presence of a higher power. For many, the awe of being outdoors in the first place is in delighting at one's smallness in the grand scheme. And what a powerful spiritual image does a creature that is able to fly through the actual heavens, carrying the word of God along on his travels, create.

The work of the Jack Miner Bird Sanctuary continues to this day, even though Miner has been gone for many years. Ducks and geese are banded and released by staff biologists, and the sanctuary continues to be supported by private donation. In recent years, Miner bands have been placed on as many as 1,000 ducks and more than 500 geese, and meticulous records are kept of where bands are recovered. Annually, bands are returned from as many as twenty or more states. The actual bands are highly collectible, since the odds of any individual hunter collecting one are obviously very slim. If you pay attention, you'll see Miner bands auctioned off at fund-raising banquets, or sold privately, where they command high prices.

Regardless of the monetary worth of the Miner bands or the notoriety that Miner enjoyed, among those of us who gather in garages and cellars and motels and duck blinds and duck camps each fall, Miner's legacy is a priceless gift. It is nothing more than a matter of opinion whether or not he is the patron saint of our sport. Then again, maybe the beauty of duck and goose hunting is that the traditions of the sport don't need a hero anyway. The birds know no boundaries, and at best belong to any of us only seasonally. But to anyone who has paused to wonder at a flight of ducks making their way across autumn skies or has gathered with friends to carry out a fall ritual, the memory of Wild Goose Jack is a fine and noble way to look forward to another season.

ABBY

"She takes just like a woman...but she breaks just like a little girl."
—Bob Dylan

I have done a pretty fair amount of duck hunting over recent seasons, and while I have some hunting friends and acquaintances, more and more these days I duck hunt alone. I'm not what you would call a loner, but some years ago I hunted with a partner, and for about ten years we were as inseparable as duck hunters got. It was one of those great ducking relationships that halved the work and expense, and more than doubled the fun. We thought so much alike that at times I'd pick up the phone to dial it, and my partner would be at the other end, having just placed a call to me, but having not yet heard a ring. Season after season we were on the same wavelength about when we needed to work, what gear we needed to buy, and when it was time to call in sick. One of us rarely hunted without the other.

Then my partner got almost maniacally involved in a new business, and at about that time I was forced to give up my enjoyable, but almost nomadic, form of existence that allowed me to hunt and fish in a couple of states and on a couple of continents each year. As my partner's business grew, I was forced to move east, and we drifted apart; a few years ago even the Christmas cards stopped. Mutual friends tell me my old partner had actually quit duck hunting altogether shortly after our last season together. Apparently, he is now big into rockhounding, and—although he still does a little fishing—he looks for rocks most weekends with his kids. How could anyone who has ever spent sleepless days and weeks and months chasing ducks just stop? I'd rather lose a limb than stop chasing ducks. I never live bigger or go at life harder than during duck season. Recall the chill you feel when you first become aware of a flight of whistling ducks' wings landing in your decoys in the predawn blackness with a swish as they touch down. Do you think you could ever feel that same chill looking at a piece of quartz?

But I still have the memories from those partnered years—the idle hours spent on duck-less days in blinds good and bad all over the Middle West, from ice-cold diver blinds in Minnesota to prairie pothole outings in the Dakotas—to a road trip to Texas that left us both with a lifetime of memories of snow geese in the fog. We suffered boats that leaked, vehicles that quit, motors that balked, decoys that sank, money that ran out, and—season after season—we shared rooms, thermoses, shotgun shells, and dry socks. If I brought the boat, he brought the dog, and if I forgot the oars, he had a spare set.

The last memory I have of a hunt together is from a time when I suspect that Jimmy Carter was still president, or maybe early in the Reagan years. The two of us were heading for home on a lonely blacktop road in my battered Ford truck. Heavy, gray skies darkened the afternoon, and the dusting of dry snow that lay on the blacktop left rolling white plumes in our wake. Merle Haggard explained away his vices on the cassette. We ate bean dip from an open container on the dashboard and potato chips from a bag on the bench seat, washing both down with the dregs of the morning's cold coffee. We had limits of drake mallards and pintails in the back of the truck, and even though it was well below 30 degrees, the truck windows were cranked well down—the freezing fresh air helping to keep us awake for the trip home. We laughed, talked about how the birds had decoyed, and drove away the afternoon. I have been on hundreds of duck hunts in the years that have followed, but I have never felt as free as I did that day. That was a lot of years ago.

This past spring I was painting decoys in the garage, and my young daughter, Abby, happened by to inquire as to what I was doing. I explained about decoy painting and what the decoys did and the like, and thought that would be the last I'd hear about duck hunting from her. But almost unbelievably, as the summer progressed into early autumn, there were more and more questions and a real expression of interest on

Abby's part. I had been looking toward another duck season alone, but here a new partner was appearing right under my feet. At eight, she was too young to shoot, but I made preparations to at least take her along with me, envisioning one of those father-daughter bonding days that I hoped to remember with crystal clarity as my family huddles around my deathbed someday in the hopefully damned distant future. Paging through the gear catalogs I scour for myself anyway, I gradually acquired some little knee boots and a pint-size camouflage outfit, and then tucked them away.

Meanwhile I began to slip duck hunting into Abby's little life like double agents slip knockout pills into the drinks of other double agents in the spy movies. We talked about the boat and the marsh, and about putting out and picking up decoys, and she laughed when I told her the smell of the mud would curl her nose. We both giggled when I threw a decoy into the tub one evening at bath time. Saturday morning cartoons gradually began to alternate with Saturday morning outdoor programming. Rides to soccer games and piano lessons featured short lessons on the pintail whistle. After mandatory removal of bubble gum, we explored the basics of the feeding call. Friends who hunt with their children cautioned me to keep lessons short and learning fun, so I did. When I encountered resistance or boredom, I left well enough alone.

We looked through duck identification books and it wasn't long before Abby—a pretty bright kid—could tell the difference between a wigeon and a gadwall, or a bluebill and a ring-neck, by keying in on the important details that separated the species. If I saw ducks in a roadside ditch, I'd usually stop and offer a pop quiz on what we were looking at. Abby usually got them right. She was a very quick study, and her sharp mind and quick wit reminded me of the story about the schoolteacher relating "The Three Little Pigs" to her second-grade class.

As you may recall, the first pig decides to build his house from straw, and soon goes into the hardware store to purchase bundles of straw for the construction. The pig asks the hardware store owner if he may buy some straw from him. At this point in the story, the teacher asked the class, "And what do you think the man at the hardware store said to the first little pig when he asked to buy the straw?"

A hand shoots up in the front row and little Sally blurts out, "Holy shit, a talking pig!"

Abby is a talking pig kind of kid. I'm sure when I'm not watching she runs with scissors or rips the Do Not Remove Under Penalty of Law tags off the couch cushions. She prefers to go barefoot even in the dead of winter, and has a gap between her front teeth and a sparkle in her eye that melts my heart.

Finally, the duck season started, but our father-daughter hunt was preempted by activities that one might expect would foil hunting plans if you were eight years old. There was a birthday party or maybe two, Halloween, soccer, and practice for a school play. I waited patiently. There were so many activities that I began to think they were excuses and that she'd lost interest. But I knew I still had the green light when several times Abby came into our cluttered back storage room and, sitting on the clothes dryer, kept me company while I cleaned ducks I had taken on my own outings. She stroked the birds, and would pick brightly colored speculum feathers from a green-winged teal, or the curled tail from a drake mallard, and admire them. Her brown eyes lit with curiosity as she touched the ducks' bills, and she giggled as she poked at the webbing of their feet. We talked about hiding her long blond hair underneath her camouflage cap, and I was thrilled to see her enjoy our duck-cleaning encounters. I was as proud as I could be, since she seemed to show not only her usual eight-year-old silliness, but curiosity and respect for the birds as well.

A week later we packed her duffel bag, and heeding earlier advice from friends, I packed all kinds of things that I thought would entertain Abby in the car and in the duck blind. I had books, electronic games, hot chocolate, hand heaters, and candy. I had packed a step stool, so that she would be able to see everything out of the blind. Afraid she'd be cold, even though weather predictions were for morning temperatures in the fifties, I had enough mittens and gloves and fleece and neck warmers that she would be able to handle anything short of the Iditarod. We were only going to be out for three or four hours—how bored or cold could she get?

Through the packing process of an hour or so on the evening of our departure, Abby strutted about the house, clearly proud to be going duck hunting. We were going to stay the night in a very plain motel near our marsh. At one point, my wife made a sideways comment about the cleanliness of the place, and Abby—though she had not been there herself yet—defended the place as if it were Camelot. In fact, her enthusiasm manifested itself to the stage that I had to rein her in just a little when she made a flip comment to a non-hunting neighbor lady who popped by. The neighbor wished us, and specifically Abby, good luck, and said she hoped we'd "catch a lot of ducks."

Abby corrected her, but was just a little too flip when she crossed her arms and told our neighbor lady, "We don't catch ducks. We shoot ducks!"

After our neighbor had closed the door behind her, and before she had made it to the front gate, Abby and I were having a calm but one-sided discussion. I explained that, first, she was going to accompany me duck hunting. Second, we were going to have fun together. Third, she was not to present herself to Mrs. Fillipaster as an authority on waterfowl quite yet.

I was trying to be a disciplinarian, but got a kick out of Abby's zeal for the outing and had a hard time keeping a straight face during my little lecture. I was reminded of a story about my friend Tom and his daughter. Tom is a lifelong, dyed-in-the-wool fly fisherman who not only lives on a beautiful piece of trout water in Montana, but has fished with a fly just about everywhere you can do so. In his book *Live Water*, he recalled that his daughter once heard some playground companion say something about "the F word." Assuming the F word was fishing, Tom's daughter later proclaimed, to some houseguests Tom didn't know very well, that "all my father cares about is the F word. When he is not doing it, he is reading about it."

We packed the truck, and as I pecked my wife on the cheek she told me to be careful. A sudden thumping across the ceiling ended as Abby came bounding down the stairway, her brown eyes flashing and her blond hair trailing in her wake. She had her teddy bear under her arm.

"I have Brownie, so now we can go," she stated. I should have just left well enough alone and accepted the teddy bear's company as part of the deal, but I rolled my eyes at my wife, and Abby caught me doing it. A sheepish look grew across her face and her cheeks flashed red. I could see her caught in that chasm that separates children, who are pushed so hard to be grown up in these fast-paced times, from the kids they really are. We hopped in the truck and were off into the night.

Along the way, Abby and I talked about school and I teased her about the boys in her class. We laughed about road signs for towns with silly names like Lorain and Euclid, and made up potty-mouthed poems about them. I realized I had not prepared her for how loud the shotgun was. She finished that discussion with a series of repetitions of, "This loud?" Each question was followed by "Boom," screamed in a louder and louder voice until she was at the top of her range. I told her she'd probably be startled, but not too scared.

The following morning dawned clear and calm, and I let Abby sleep with Brownie while I made coffee, hot chocolate, and breakfast preparations. When all was done, except to get her dressed, I rousted her out of bed and got her suited up. Before long, we were making our way to the marsh. The short walk in and the decoy placement went without a hitch, and I had Abby place a few special decoys. Soon we were in the blind with time to spare before the appointed shooting hour. Sure that we'd see thousands and thousands of blackbirds, I foreshadowed that possibility for Abby. I also told her to keep a sharp eye out for swans, as I knew we'd see two or three. This was part of my sage guide routine, and I laid that groundwork so I could be right about these things later.

As the sky brightened little by little and shooting became legal, there were ducks in the air in good numbers, and Abby divided her time between standing on her stool and sitting in the blind. I called out duck species as birds crossed over. Several ducks lit in the decoy spread, but I did not shoot a duck in the predawn, thinking it best to wait until daylight would help put the whole ducks-decoys-

shooting picture together for Abby. Selfishly, I made mental notes that I had let more than half a dozen easily killable birds float right through the decoy spread.

Ten minutes later, Abby was sipping hot chocolate and I was removing my jacket when the blackbirds came pouring over us in an endless, rolling wave, at times giving the impression that the whole marsh was covered by a black, billowing sheet. This caught Abby's attention, and she commented that there were a lot of them.

Not two minutes after that, the two worst words I could ever hear in a duck blind came out of my darling daughter's mouth. "I'm bored," she said.

"Bored?" I asked. "How can you be bored? We have been in this blind for a grand total of forty-five minutes," I said, as I pulled back my cuff to look at my watch with disbelief.

"Play some of your games or read one of the books in

your backpack," I encouraged. It was not yet eight o'clock in the morning.

"I didn't bring them," Abby replied. "I didn't think I'd want to have them with me," she said, picking small flakes of purple polish off her fingernails.

I could feel the morning unraveling, and I steeled myself. Like the saying about the wrath of a woman scorned, there is no rest from a child bored. The whining will wear you down like no other torture imaginable, and in a car or a closed space like a duck blind there is no escape. I scanned the skies and called at a flock of distant mallards, determined to at least get some quick shooting before this was all over. A threesome of mallards worked the spread, and as they sailed inside the 200-yard mark I whispered to Abby to get up on her stool so she could watch. I blew a landing call, dragging out the *quuaaack, quuaack, quuaaack* notes, and three pairs of wings set. Hunched over, I wrapped a hand around the forearm of my gun, and as the birds were just seventy yards out, lined up for the space in the decoys we'd laid for them, I heard a loud bang. Then a clang and a clunk. Abby had accidentally brushed the steel thermos off the shelf in the blind and onto the wooden floor. The mallards towered away, and Abby smirked and fixed her gaze on the top of her boots.

The next twenty minutes passed painfully, as Abby repeatedly expressed her boredom and made a comment that she was ready to leave anytime. She wiggled and twisted and writhed in her seat on the bench of the blind in the same way she does on a pew in church. This same set of fidgeting motion—now under a camouflage jacket—was what I normally see out of her when she is wearing her Sunday best.

"Dad, I'm ready to leave," she said again, emphasizing the "I."

I calmly informed her that she had signed on for the whole tour and that she needed to just tough things out a little longer. It wasn't 8:30 yet, and she had the whole day ahead of her. But kids work in the present. I knew I needed to get her out of there soon or run the risk that her lasting memory of duck hunting would be that it was boring. I worked the jerk string and scanned the skies.

Finally, a drake mallard sailed in, and as I tried to land him with feeding chatter punctuated with a few soft quacks, I again told Abby to carefully stand up so she could watch things happen. The greenhead locked his wings, made one short downwind turn over the spread, and then sailed toward the center of the decoys. I stood up, clicked the safety off, and cartwheeled the drake right over the hole in the decoys. Thankfully, he fell right into the center of the blocks, gray breast up and orange feet weakly waving. There was no need for a follow-up shot or a neck-wringing retrieve, two things that are occasionally part of duck hunting that I realized I was not equipped to explain to my daughter quite yet.

As the ripples from the mallard's fall dissipated across the water, the sudden silence that always follows ducks falling to a gunshot was broken by a sharp voice that asked,

"Did we get him?"

"Yes we did, honey," I replied to the same person who, moments ago, was making much ado about the fact that she was bored, she was tired, and she wanted to leave. Now she was a team player, and *we* had a duck in the bag. Go figure.

Shortly thereafter we packed up the decoys and, after a short water fight, started the process of making our way home. After an hour or so in the car, I asked Abby if she'd had a good time, and if she'd like to go again. Not getting a reply, I glanced up into the rearview mirror. Stretched out across the back seat, she was fast asleep under a blanket she'd made out of her hunting parka. Brownie the teddy bear was tucked under her arm, and wisps of her blond hair fell across Brownie's stubby, stuffed arms.

I don't know if I'll make Abby into a hunting partner or if she'll make me into a doting father first, but driving home I was feeling free once again, and I rolled down the window and let in some fresh air.

RATACZAK '02

Chapter Fourteen

KNOW WHEN TO
SAY WHEN

"Neither the market shooter nor the non-professional gunner
has sufficient self-control to stop shooting when he has
killed a fair bag of birds."
—George Bird Grinnell, *American Duck Shooting*

I have been awfully fortunate in a relatively short waterfowling career, and have had the chance to hunt not only
in quite a few states, but in a few foreign countries as
well. I talk here at home with a lot of "regular guys" who will
never have the chance to hunt in Mexico or Argentina.
Although I think I have a few interesting stories to tell, I'd just
as soon not talk about it with most of my usual hunting
crowd. A lot of guys have the impression that hunting in
another country is just such a dropkick easy deal that it is as
simple as Pedro rolling out the red carpet for you. Then you
are free to shoot all the birds you want, and you never have to
work for them, much less retrieve them. After another epic

hunt, it is all about rolling back to the hacienda to wait in the shade until you are called upon again to display your shooting prowess. Yeah, and I'm the king of Siam.

Sporting writers often add fuel to this fire, and call these far-off places the "land of milk and honey." These magazine guys often shoot triples on decoying birds without getting a hair on their head out of place; sing the praises of the extended magazine tube; are welcomed with open arms by Pedro, Juan, or whomever; and always give bunches of ducks to the poor or the needy. Yes, there are a lot of ducks, but it isn't usually that easy.

I was picked up at the tiny terminal of a small town in Argentina one August not too long ago, and after a butt-numbing ride in a rancher's stiff-springed Toyota, found myself approaching the sprawling yard of an estancia home in Argentina's corn belt, south of Buenos Aires. I had come to see this duck hunt because I had heard it was a good one. Not only was this Argentina's corn belt, but it was her rain belt too, and each winter the latter reportedly conspired to flood the former, making ducks concentrate—as they are wont to do when they are offered one-stop shopping for food and water. We rolled up the long gravel drive, and there in the yard were displayed 150 some ducks of about three different varieties that two gentlemen from a southern state of the U.S. had just killed that morning. The ducks were laid out in a tableau of the sort you see in European game parades: a duck every two feet, laid neatly in rows of ten or twelve, and perhaps fifteen rows deep. The two men were busily snapping pictures of one another, taking turns posing behind the ducks, then crouching to get all of the ducks in the frame, with the house in the background.

✦ ✦ ✦

That evening, we had drinks together, and as the men recounted the day's action it came out in the conversation that one of them had had just mediocre shooting that morning, and that the other was responsible for the lion's share of the birds. He had killed more than 115 birds himself in a little more than two hours. This is, of course, quite legal, or from the standpoint of the law in the third world, not at all an issue. In many provinces of Argentina there are no written daily limits, and the day's take is often governed by transportation—the number of ducks you can transport from field to home. This can easily be justified based on the number of decoy setters, bird picker-uppers, and hangers-on who can fit into the bed of a truck. That doesn't really matter, since game enforcement in Latin America is often nonexistent.

But my argument is not about the legality of this issue. The question is, at what point is enough truly enough? At what stage does the hunter say, "I quit. I don't want to kill any more ducks on this hunt."

When does a decoying duck quit becoming part of a very serious, sacred transaction between hunter and hunted and become number forty-eight? What makes us go to bed as fathers and husbands and regular guys, and wake up as a Lord Ripon wanna-be? At what stage does duck hunting become duck shooting, and at what stage does duck shooting just become duck killing?

I will not preach, and you won't find me casting the first stone either. I have been on some tremendous duck hunts in South America, have seen the skies black with wild ducks, and have killed more than my share of them on a given day. But I look back now and I am not only saddened, but also ashamed. Why didn't it occur to me before the fact that it was not necessary to kill a big bag? Perhaps it is a situation not unlike being caught smoking cigarettes as a youngster. "Sure, go ahead and smoke," said your parents or your track coach. "As a matter of fact, why don't you sit right down here and smoke this whole pack?" Maybe the rebound from overindulgence is the key to learning the lesson.

At the risk of toppling off of my lofty soapbox, why go in the first place, and how much is enough? When you pay money to hunt with a guide in Arkansas, you are really just a shooter, aren't you? You don't scout, and you usually don't set decoys or retrieve downed birds; the guide handles all of that for you. The same is true in Mexico or Canada; there's just potential for a bigger bag north or south of the border. I just heard from an acquaintance the other day about two men who killed 163 redheads between them on one morning in Mexico. One of them reportedly—or sheepishly—said, "Well, we are big Ducks Unlimited donors." Like that makes a difference. They might as well have said, "We were fresh out of passenger pigeons."

In contrast, I was once on a hunt in Argentina with an officer from a noted waterfowl conservation organization who had truly devoted his life to doing good works for waterfowl in North America. He had such trouble contemplating the prospect of shooting a lot of ducks in a day—say thirty or forty—that I'm convinced he psyched himself into a shooting slump to avoid the possibility of doing so. On one morning in particular, he had birds decoy with total abandon for two hours, and he missed shot after shot after shot—most of them in the fifteen-yard range. Later he attributed his shooting trouble to lifting his head off the stock, commonly called "peeking." I think he really had had a peek at his conscience. But what is it that triggers any of us to change from the attitude of "more is better" to "I've just had enough"?

I have a good friend from Minnesota who once was a gung-ho duck hunter, as gung-ho as I ever saw. This guy had a basement full of decoys, about four boats, and a big Labrador that was so well conformed that—when wet—it looked like a black jaguar. My friend was a contest-quality duck caller. He painted decoys, trained his dog, and fixed his boats all summer, and he about gave everything he had every fall to hunt ducks. He did this for years, and could kill a limit of ducks in a rain barrel, or so it seemed. He always hunted public land, or asked permission, and he never had a lease or a regular spot when he was hunting actively. He killed limit after limit after limit of ducks for days on end. He worked in the afternoons and evenings, and slept in the car on his dinner break. I still recall photos I saw of him some years ago—grinning in front of his hunting rig, a bouquet of mallards in each hand. Then one day he just quit.

He told me some years later that he had taken duck hunting as far as he could—that he had just gotten so good at hunting ducks that all it had become for him was an exercise in sleep deprivation. And it all came down to getting the "number" each day. If the limit was four, he'd get four; if it was five, he'd get five. He scouted and scouted and scouted some more so he would always have options, and if they didn't pan out, he'd jump-shoot his ducks on other places he had scouted too. He told me this without a sliver of egotism, because he knew I knew he was as good as he said he was. I had seen it firsthand.

Since then, my friend has taken up upland bird hunting, and he has a string of impeccably behaved pointing dogs in kennels at his house. If he offered, you'd take any one of his six or eight dogs in a minute. He hunts grouse and woodcock now exclusively, and hasn't shot at a duck in at least ten years. He guides a little, more for company than for money, and could not care less about shooting all the birds the law allows him on any given day. In fact, he won't shoot a bird that is not pointed, and pointed well, and—best of all—he

seems content. Why the change? Maybe he finally got to the edge, got tired of the numbers game, and didn't like the person he saw in the looking glass every morning.

For many, shooting a mass of ducks in a far-off land is not an issue, as many will likely not make the long trip to Argentina or Mexico. Even on a guided hunt in the United States or Canada, shooting over limits is impossible, since guides won't risk fines or their reputation so you can shoot a few extra birds. Hunting every day of the season isn't an option for most of us who try to remain gainfully employed or have families. But if you do get a chance to travel, try to approach a trip as a chance to experience a different culture. Value a hunt in Mexico as a chance to see some of Mexico and do some shooting outside your regular season. Don't get so focused on killing ducks that you forget to smell the roses while you are there. Do the same in your boat or blind at home. If you lose a cripple, absolutely count it as being in the daily bag. Try to shoot only the drakes, regardless of where you stand about this from a conservation perspective. At a bare minimum, you have to admit it is worth doing for the fact that drakes look better in your pictures.

Hunt with a camera; use it when it's not your turn to shoot incoming birds. You'd be surprised at how much less you'll suffer between duck seasons if you have some good photos to prompt your memories of the fall. Take action photos too—not just grip-and-grin shots of your buddy holding up dead ducks. We all mature as hunters, as evidenced by so many older hunters who could not care less about shooting anything, but who wouldn't miss the day in the blind or the weekend in camp. You'll likely find that toning down the urge to get to a limit takes the pressure off. It also tends, over time, to produce a sort of quiet self-respect within you, which will lead to great respect from other hunters. As you focus less on knocking down all the birds the law allows, wherever you may be, you'll also have more time to see and absorb fully all of the details that make up the hunt itself.

Chapter Fifteen

PERMISSION

For the diving duck specialist, permission is not usually a big issue, as rivers and large lakes across the country are very often quite public and are equipped with ready access. Meanwhile, club hunters, leaseholders, or property owners are generally not concerned with privacy or elbowroom. But for the freelancer, and especially the puddle duck hunter, getting onto small marshes and potholes, or into grainfields, is vital to the pursuit of those species of ducks that frequent shallow water and walk on terra firma. True, there is a lot of public access hunting in this country, but to really get to the good stuff—and, more important, to get away from the growing horde of our camouflaged comrades—you are going to have to ask permission.

Not having a lot of access to private duck hunting until quite recently, I grew up poking around for my ducks and hunting for public ground. I consider myself at least well versed in asking permission for duck hunting. If getting on farms was something they kept records of, like a lifetime batting average, I was probably about as successful as the next guy. But over the years it seems like I have gotten on a lot of farms and have enjoyed some very memorable duck hunts inside private gates. However, the days of just seeing a bunch of ducks pitch into a rural marsh, then driving into a farmer's driveway to ask permission and having "yes" be the dropkick answer are largely over, except in a few lightly populated states or in some of the Canadian provinces where permission is still liberal. I don't have all of the answers, but "getting on" privately held ground is an increasingly difficult, but not impossible proposition.

Sadly, there are incidents in the news that have hurt all hunters, and in some cases hunters have hurt themselves. Everyone has likely read a story over the years about a rifle-toting idiot who shot a cow and let it lie in a pasture, only to be found by a farmer later. You need only look at rural road signs to be chagrined by other hunters' behavior. I'll make a deal here: Next time you are out scouting, count the bullet holes in the road signs you pass and mail me a nickel for every one you count. It is easy for you and I to say it is those "other" hunters, the "slob" hunters, but every time you step into a farmer's yard, you stand to get painted with the same brush as the cow killers and the sign shooters. Further—and right or wrong—violent crime and school shootings can also work to tip the scales against you. Sadly, some landowners have had bad experiences with hunters in the past, and their answer is, and always will be, that you will have to look elsewhere.

Fortunately, farmers as a group are spawned from other farmers, and you are dealing with people from rural backgrounds who understand that gun issues are largely urban problems. Most farmers and farm families lead lives that are far closer to the land than those of any other segment of the population. This seems simplistic, but farmers are more in touch with issues of hunting and gathering, land stewardship, conservation, and even life and death. Many of the nation's farmers raise livestock, as well as grain, and they see animals die cruelly in winter storms or see them accidentally hung in wire fences. They take animals to slaughterhouses, they know how the food chain works, and they know that the meat in your grocer's freezer was on the hoof just precious days earlier. Those who have not had bad experiences with hunters who may have preceded you are generally apt to be sympathetic to sincere hunters who appreciate access to their land, and who want to continue the tradition of hunting wild game as a way to reconnect with the land themselves.

When it gets down to the brass tacks of asking a landowner about the land you are interested in hunting, you must think like a salesman; if you really want to add a lot of super spots to your hunting menu, add a car dealer to your group. Some of the best hunts I have been on were with two friends, one of whom was John, an honest-faced Chevrolet dealer. On road trips to the prairie states, we'd scout for ducks and then send John to the door to ask permission. It did not matter if there were No Hunting signs on every phone pole on the property, mean dogs in the yard, or animal rights bumper stickers on every car in the driveway; this guy would get us in the door, and he'd almost always make a friend too. I often joked that we could have financed those trips by having John sell encyclopedias to the farmers as he asked permission from them. John also taught me to keep some standard gift items in the vehicle; if we gained permission, we could go right back to the farmhouse—after the hunt—and leave a jar of maple syrup, a bottle of wine, or some wild rice as a thank-you.

This salesman attitude may sound almost deceitful, and I don't want to state my case as if I promote pulling the wool over the eyes of America's farmers, but the simple fact is that you are trying to make a sale. Simply, you are selling the landowner on allowing you access to his property. One of you will close the deal. Either you will get on the land, or he will send you away to look for somewhere else to hunt. As the office manager says in the cult movie *Glenngary Glen Ross,* "Always be closing."

I had a boss at a fishing lodge in Alaska when I was younger. This guy—a real go-getter—runs one of Alaska's top sport fishing lodges to this day. His clientele is made up of scions of industry, finance, banking, and technology in this country. My employer never got out of high school. But, when I worked for him, I noticed that at every opportunity he read every newspaper, current events magazine, and financial magazine he could get his hands on, so that he was able to converse with his fishing clients on their level. He knew that if he had some basic knowledge of a topic, and the courage and ability to ask a thoughtful question, the client he was guiding would usually be happy to reply. Then, the client would just be happy to continue talking about himself, which is human nature. In either case, the lodge owner viewed this as a customer service, although I'm sure that, as a by-product, he learned a little something along the way.

The fishermen, meanwhile, felt good about the lodge owner's personal interest in them.

I relate this story because there are parallels for us here as we plan to approach a landowner. This is not to say that you should subscribe to *Pork Producer* or memorize current articles from *The Field Corn Journal*, but you should at the very least be familiar with the area. Statistically, the average farmer in the United States is white, fifty-three years old, and married. Know at least what crops these men are likely to have in their fields. Know whether the area is ahead or behind on annual rainfall—if you are duck hunting, you are listening to the weather anyway. And don't punch the radio buttons the next time the commodities news is broadcast; instead, listen. You might learn something about July corn or September wheat. Also, know what your Major League Baseball team did last night. These are issues that may be important to a landowner, and they are just part of knowing your audience and being a smart and ready conversationalist. This kind of thing is not much different from the preparation work your wife does with you in the car on the way to a dinner party. Also, look around the yard as you pull in. See any bicycles or other toys? If so, he has children, and if you do, too, there is some common ground. Notice if there is a garden, and see what is planted in it. Is there a fishing boat around? If so, you may talk about fishing or cars or whatever.

Meanwhile, put yourself in the farmer's shoes. What if a total stranger showed up unannounced at your door and asked to pick flowers or vegetables from your garden? Whether you live in a rural location or in a town or in the suburbs, would you let him? Were you planning to pick the flowers yourself? Were you saving the vegetables for your niece who is coming to pick them next week? Would you trust this complete stranger to just walk onto your land and do what he wants? Maybe the landowner is saving the spot for a cousin or a doctor friend from town. These are both answers I have heard before. In those cases I usually ask the doctor's name or the cousin's name, and tell the landowner I will call them and see if they'd like some company, and would that be OK? You have to think differently, depending on whether you are a local or an out-of-towner. If this is a spot you'd like to work into your seasonal repertoire, you have time to work on a landowner. If you are just in his area for a week, and he says no for one reason another, tell him you are from another state and ask if he can point you in a general direction of good duck concentrations. Be empathetic to the landowner's situation.

By all means, make sure your permission asking is happening before or after the harvest of whatever this landowner is harvesting. The busiest and most stressful time of year for farmers is during their harvest. They will rarely give you the time of day when they are picking anything, and they need rest and relaxation during this time. Leave them alone then. The focus of their lives is to get the crops out of the ground, whether it is rice or soybeans or corn. This is doubly true in areas where harsh winters pull the seasonal curtain down in a hurry. And don't ask to dig pits. Farmers hate pit blinds. If you ask enough farmers, I promise you will find one who has had at least one bad pit blind experience. Talking about it just cuts down on your chances of getting on. With the advent of lie-down, chair-style blinds, pits are not necessary anyway, so if the farmer asks about pit blinds specifically, be sure to tell him you want to hunt the first floor and not dig the basement.

When you show up at the door, either before the hunting season or during it, cut down or at least minimize the camouflage gear. The men don't usually care, but wives and children may be put off by it, and they may choose not to answer the door at all. If you have a dog or dogs in the vehicle, leave them in the vehicle. Nothing will queer your chances of hunting a farmer's spot like a big dogfight in the front yard, and there are—more often than not—dogs at every farm. Once someone answers the door, be pleasant, brief, and respectful of their time. If the family looks like they are all running out the door on an errand, ask quickly or tell them you'll stop back later. If you are invited in for coffee, by all means go in, and then act as you would if you were a houseguest anywhere. I once stopped at a farm, and after inquiring at the house if I could speak with the landowner, was directed to a machine shed located several hundred yards from the house. The radio was blaring, and as I walked into the cavernous shed I found the landowner lying on a cold concrete floor under a tractor, banging on a hitch plate of some sort. I stopped next to the frame of the red, monster tractor, close to where his legs and feet extended out from under the belly of the machine.

"Hello there," I said in my most sincere voice.

No reply.

"Good morning. Have you got a minute?" I tried again.

Nothing.

I then got down on all fours and looked under the tractor, but could not really see the man, as the top half of his body was lost in the white glare of his shop light—the kind with the bulb enclosed in a little mesh cage.

I then lay down on my back and scrunched under the tractor a little farther myself, where I could now at least see the man. He had on a suit of green coveralls and had a big crescent wrench in one hand and a big hammer in the other. He was whacking on a wallet-sized steel plate. I could tell he was not getting a free swing at the plate, since holding the wrench was shortening his hammer blows.

"Let me hold that for you," I said.

He did not reply, but he loosened his grip on the wrench and I slid my hand down the handle. He then shifted his weight, and lying on his side began clanging on the plate with much more force. "I have been trying *[clang]* to get this *[clang]* son of a bitch *[clang]* off for damned near an hour *[clang, clang, clonk]*. There, finally," he said.

Then, in a gruff voice, "Who are you?"

As I crawled out from under the tractor, I explained who I was, where I was from, and that I was interested in hunting the large marsh located on the property he owned that was not contiguous with his farm and outbuildings. I told him I was only interested in hunting ducks, and that I had hunted on a lot of farm property before, was respectful of it, and would leave gates as I found them and the like. When he did not reply, I added that I knew several folks locally that he could talk to who would be willing to vouch for my character.

He relented and let me know I was free to go ahead, but not until after we had talked about baseball, weather, college football, and a couple of different businesses we were familiar with. It was just pleasant talk, and while I was selling this man on my safety and competence, I found it was also pleasant to talk with him. Like many landowners, he was a regular guy, with bills to pay and problems and the need to just blow off a little steam from time to time. I asked him to hunt along with me, but he was not interested.

I ended the conversation by telling him when the season would open and what vehicle I'd be driving. I also offered to drop some ducks off for him if I was successful. He was a big, easygoing guy, and I may have gotten the chance to hunt his place if he had just opened the door to the house in the first place. But I like to believe he thought that any guy who would lie on a floor and hold a complete stranger's wrench could not be all bad.

✦ ✦ ✦

No matter how asking permission goes for you, do all hunters a favor and leave every landowner conversation on a good note. Even if you are rejected, say something like, "Thanks anyway for taking the time to talk with me. I appreciate that you let your cousin [dentist, doctor, friend, etc.] on your land. Helpful landowners are becoming increasingly difficult to come by, and I'm happy to have met someone who lets folks hunt on their land. Here is my name and phone number in case any possibility would come up." Leaving contact information has paid off for me only twice in twenty-some years, but in both cases the hunts they provided were wildly successful and were of the "come now, the ducks are here in a big way" variety. Those are the kind of calls that keep you up nights thinking about them.

If you establish a relationship with a farmer, don't forget to add him to your Christmas card list, just as you likely do with other friends and acquaintances. I'm always astonished at hunters who do nothing for a landowner year in and year out, yet show up at his door each season looking for ready access. These are the same guys who spend weeks and weeks getting ready for the season. Put a little of your catalog shopping time into landowner relations. Getting and keeping permission has got to be a two-way street, and we all need to cooperate with and appreciate landowners in order to continue to allow more closed gates to open for all of us.

Chapter Sixteen

MERGANSER DECOYS

I was up about four o'clock the other morning and had the coffeemaker running shortly thereafter. I dressed in the dark and looked through the frosted windowpane at the thermometer, which held steady at 25 degrees. I then quietly slipped out the back door to the porch to assess the weather conditions in person before picking up my final layer of clothing off the hook for the day. Having loaded decoys the night before, I packed a stool, my gun case, and odds and ends in the front of the truck, and started the engine to let it idle and begin the defrosting process. I was right on time—I always like to start a morning's duck hunting right on time—and had agreed to meet Howard at five at a gas station that was an honest forty minutes from home.

Meanwhile my wife was fast asleep. She is used to my early morning departures, but she has remained insistent that I say a personal good-bye before leaving. I used to fudge it, and tell her later that I had said good-bye when I really had not. I figured, hell, she's half asleep; she'll never know.

Herb Alpert could play a solo in the bedroom and I wouldn't wake up if our roles were reversed. But my wife knows; all wives know these things. They sleep different than men, and are aware of their husband's whereabouts even in sleep. Now I just make time in my routine to tell her I'm off.

Although I was stocking footed, the swish of the heavy Cordura on my overalls announced my arrival as I climbed the stairs. Then I stood next to the bed and advised of my imminent departure. "Drive carefully," she replied.

On the way out of the leaf-paved driveway and down our dark street, it dawned on me just how ironic it was that she was concerned for my safety on the road, when driving empty roads in the predawn hours during the duck season is about as safe a time as there is on any road. You aren't going to get hit by another car—there are rarely other cars around. You might see a bakery truck on a delivery run, but that is about it.

I was in fact on my way to hunt a duck blind reported to be in a backwater of a river system big enough to handle barge traffic. To get to the spot supposedly required launching a boat in a small marina, followed by a run of three miles or so in this morning's below-freezing cold. Of course, we'd be running the boat in the dark, and very likely there would be some skim ice along the way, plus logs or any other obstacles that might be floating down the river. I was going to do this with a guy I had never met, except on the Internet.

I don't think I was the last guy on my street to get a computer at home, but I was later to the game than I would have liked to have been. Like it or not, E-mail, Web sites, and all the cyber communication that goes with them are here to stay. If you are dyed-in-the-wool about anything, sooner or later you'll find a site where others can join you to talk about how avid they are too. Case in point: I was surfing around the sports information on my computer the other day and discovered there are seven sites for sepak takraw, the Asian sport of foot volleyball. I had no idea people played volleyball with their feet. It brings to mind the fairly recent joke about asking your computer to search for something ridiculous by entering something like "sex with goats," and the search engine sends back a message that states "specify type of goat."

There are many, many Web sites for the duck hunter to chat, read, rant, shop, and gather information. Many sites divide their contributors by state, so you can communicate with those in the same general area and compare notes. While much of the information can be extremely useful, I have found that much of the pleasure of being involved in the duck hunting world through the computer is in exchanging ideas with others –hearing about other hunts and other hunters on days when I cannot be in the blind myself.

Granted, it may seem of little consequence to you that some guy in Oklahoma with the computer name of Skillet Shot killed three gadwalls that morning, especially if you live two thousand miles away. Duck hunters' reports aren't quite Meg Ryan in *You've Got Mail*, but they can be fun to read. Further, the beauty of the speed of the Internet makes vast amounts of duck hunting news easy to find, so you spend little time spinning your electronic wheels. You are free to find a group of hunters who share your mind-set in a chat room, or in some other electronic forum where E-mailed answers go on display for all to see. Most folks function with nicknames or are on a first-name basis, so you may contribute in anonymity. You may communicate at will, limited only by the willingness of one or more people out in the electronic ether to answer the message you have posted. Someone is likely to either agree with your statement and give you some gratification, or dis-agree, and then you are welcome to defend your position.

The egomaniacal types don't care if anyone answers at all; they just post ideas or concepts or beliefs, then post some more. Which explains why, almost twenty years after its introduction, you see long dissertations from God of Gadwall on the ineffectiveness of steel shot, which to me is beating duck hunting's dead horse. Or you'll hear from Wisconsin Charlie that he is having a terrific season-he just had to tell someone. Meanwhile, Smiling Mallard writes, "Don't believe the birds forecast are really there, at least we ain't seein 'um."

There is also a lot of boasting, something hunters have done since the first hunts for the wooly mammoth. Ringbill Chaser, for example, just has to enter a casual discussion on duck boats to tell the free world his boat is the best and safest, because it is welded and not riveted. "After diver hunting, I ran home in eight-foot swells last week," he reported.

"Thank you very much, Captain Ahab, but it sounds to me like the best, safest boat is one where you are not at the tiller," replied Black Jack. This ended the discussion; next message.

You may also choose not to communicate at all, preferring instead to just monitor the communications of others. This is called lurking in the electronic communications trades. If you do much of this, you can read volumes—limited only by the amount of time you have to devote to it. Based on my own experience, I predict that you'll also eventually come to the conclusion that truth is indeed stranger than fiction, evidenced by some of the things I've seen, including recipes for coot, reloading formulas so dangerous that they border on terrorist directives, or instructions on illegally baiting goose fields with cheese popcorn.

But in these electronic forums you can also glean a lot from experienced hunters, and all you usually have to do is ask. Want to pour your own decoy anchors? You'll get ten or more suggestions on molds, where to get the lead, reasons for not using wheel weights, and more. What duck call to buy? Thirty or forty guys will tell you their favorites, and will give you the phone numbers for call makers and past world champions. I have seen it. Where else could you get the phone number for a world champion of anything just for the asking? I doubt you can get Picabo Street's E-mail address on a downhill skiing site, or Jack Nicklaus's home phone number on a golf forum. Duck hunting's community is different. This kind of thing has real value.

✦ ✦ ✦

As a pastime, you can also enjoy great sport in these forums. Post a nontraditional message, and the electronic sharks smell blood in the water and begin to circle. Occasionally I have posted slightly bizarre, but believable, duck hunting concepts, just for kicks and to be able to monitor the reactions. Recently I reported over the Internet that I owned some old decoys that I was preparing to paint as hooded mergansers. Further, I boasted that while I had shot plenty of ducks in my day, the merganser was plentiful, colorful, and at least edible, if not the best table fare. So why not work a little harder—I suggested—to bring them to the decoys or to become a true merganser specialist? It was not an overly impassioned argument on my part, but merely a fairly convincing trial balloon.

By my count, this message sparked twenty-seven different replies on a popular Web site's main forum. The most succinct reply was the two-word answer, "shit ducks," by someone with a password of Pump Gun, but replies ranged from a few short lines from Black Dog in Indiana who likes to shoot mergansers for his dogs' retrieving practice, to an eloquently written debate between High Baller and Curly Tail who politely argued the pros and cons of a special merganser season. Others who replied likened the merganser to a flying rat, a crow, or a coot, and most agreed that they would not go out of their way to shoot "sawbills" or eat them. Another respondent questioned the ethical dilemma

186

involved in taking legally bagged mergansers home to bury and use for fertilizing his tomato plants. My favorite was a short message by someone with an alias of Fowl Quest. He theorized that mergansers should be shot by duck hunters, who should then voluntarily supply them to prisons as food. "That would take a bite out of crime," he said.

In addition to duck hunting forums and chat rooms, there are also sites for duck callers, decoy makers, decoy collectors, and those who make floating blinds, sunken blinds, and obscure accessories. There are sites for catalogs, electronic magazines, state and federal agencies, Labrador lovers, Boykin spaniel lovers (and probably for Boykin spaniel haters)...and collectors of anything that is remotely collectible. There are hundreds of commercial sites, and then there are the auctions, which are a world unto themselves. If you have an old Herter's catalog in the house, or a rubber decoy, don't throw them away just yet. If either sits on the electronic auction block long enough, someone is apt to buy it. I talked to a fellow some weeks ago who was trying to sell eight-dozen goose decoys of the type that resemble little airport wind socks. When they didn't sell as decoys, he offered them on a general auction site, and sold them individually as lawn ornaments. They went for roughly five times their value, earning the seller enough to buy a nice new over-under. The revolution of E-commerce is moving as quickly in hunting as it is in every other facet of business.

But for all the cyber junk out there, the exponential growth, and the raging commercialism that screams at you from every electronic page, people are still people. If you exchange ideas with people long enough, you'll find that many of us are in the same boat. Exchange E-mails a little longer with someone who may live near you, and you'll literally wind up in the same boat. That's how I arranged a hunt with Howard.

The computer is letting us accomplish such things as forging friendships hundreds of times faster than real life allows. Think about how long it took to develop hunting friends you made before the computer. The meeting, the casual talking—it was like dating. You ultimately decided if this person was as serious as you were, of if he'd steal your spot. Then you made your own assessment of how safe he was, and then you'd try a hunt or two. With the computer forums, you start with a geographical area and then go through that whole process electronically. Sometimes, in a matter of a day or two, you can find yourself with a new hunting partner by the weekend.

After about a hundred E-mails back and forth and a couple of very pleasant hunts, things seem to be going well with Howard. At least he hasn't shown up at the marina with any merganser decoys.

Chapter Seventeen

THE GRAND PLAN

I took my kids to a Major League Baseball game last week and we had a fine time. We saw an evening home game and had pretty decent seats about ten rows up on the first base side. The evening was fine too. It was one of those nights that started off hot, but by the fourth inning, as the sun fell behind the towering stadium wall and the banks of lights came on, it was cool enough to put sweatshirts on the little baseball fans. I reveled in all the sights and smells and sounds of the ballpark, from the fried smell of the corn dogs to popcorn to the crack of the bat and the sound of a fastball slapping the catcher's mitt. Later I watched as orange and pink light filtered through the stands and the harsh white lights outshone the sun. By the top of the seventh, the background had fallen completely dark, and above the glowing dome of stadium light, stars began to twinkle.

It was a classic night of entertainment in America. On the drive home—with the kids, bloated on popcorn and soft drinks and nachos, sleeping in the back seat—I added up the damage. Ninety bucks for tickets; $20 or more in food and drink; $30 in souvenir programs, pennants, and a T-shirt; plus $8 to park the family wagon in the sprawling lot near the stadium. About $150, give or take a souvenir program.

Since the kids were asleep and my mind was wandering, I naturally let it wander to duck season, since that is where it usually wanders when I'm at the office or in church, or when I'm supposed to be focusing on whatever the task at hand happens to be. Certainly I wouldn't trade a ball game with my kids for all the cattails in Canada, but it dawned on me that if this is the kind of money I am spending in the name of entertainment, are we as duck hunters spending enough on our sport on a regular basis? I don't mean money that you can amortize over the seasons spent on things like super-duper waterproof jackets or dozens of decoys. We've all done the math on what it costs us to shoot a duck. Like the robot on the *Lost in Space* television series used to say, "That does not compute."

I spent some additional time contemplating this subject during a rather tedious and lengthy speech that accompanied the reopening of our local library, and later while enduring the performance of an avant-garde theater troupe that had come to town. I figure, ultimately, that anything we can do now to police our own ranks to ensure our future as waterfowlers is a prudent move. I have ruminated on this, and wish to offer my proposal, which is guaranteed to benefit us all.

The Grand Plan, which is what I call my, well, plan, is based on the premise that we are all better informed than we used to be. I know that I'm better informed than I used to be, as not more than several years ago I remained blissfully ignorant of what went on behind the scenes in duck hunting's hierarchy, including conservation organizations, government agencies, and scientific studies. For me, it generally went like this: I prepared to hunt ducks. I also went to conservation banquets, bought drink tickets, and bought duck prints. I bought camouflage caps, decals, and Labrador andirons. I bought a license and two duck stamps, wrote checks to one local waterfowl organization and one national waterfowl organization. And then I went hunting. That was it.

Now, however, with more magazines, reports, and duck hunters' Web sites, I, like so many others who consider duck hunting to be the friendly dugout in the stadium that is their life, am better informed than I ever was. I E-mail my congressman letters, the body of which I download from conservation sites. I can read fall forecasts, access long-range weather predictions and satellite maps, and read spring pond counts with the click of a mouse. Duck hunters are more involved than we have ever been. But we fail to realize that those who threaten all hunters are equally as informed. They are organized, and they read and write and organize among themselves. My Grand Plan insists that it is time to take the next step, move to the next level, and show everyone who is willing to look that we are capable of giving more to keep our passion alive. It is time to start paying daily fees for our hunting.

That is unfair, unconstitutional, and almost downright un-American, you might say. The kind of thinking that got ballroom dancing included on the list of Olympic sports. We've always enjoyed the right to hunt public waters, lakes, rivers, impoundments, and government-owned lands. Our license dollars fund these areas, they go to the purchase of wetlands, and there may well be the rightful feeling among many that we have a right to march out to any and every piece of public water that is made available to us, put out our decoys, and hunt to our heart's delight.

Before you shove a stick in my spokes, consider what would happen if there were an organized method for collecting fees for hunting on public land on a national level. What would happen if the program was so structured that we could use the funds to purchase further wetland areas? Imagine if it were just $2 or $3 per day. How much good could we do for ourselves? Wouldn't it be great for duck hunters to be able to face the rest of the world and say, "Look what we have done with our money. Not only do we contribute in the form of donations, license fees, and taxes on sporting goods, but also we have levied a tax on ourselves. We are buying our own wetlands—over and above the federal government, beyond the conservation organizations, and beyond the state areas." The Grand Plan can deliver all this and much, much more for the price of a corn dog each hunting day.

Consider a state with high hunter participation, like Arkansas, California, or Minnesota. Imagine the funds that could be generated with more than 100,000 duck hunters paying $3 for each day spent in the marsh. In three to five years, the Grand Plan could buy and preserve hundreds and thousands of acres of habitat. Let's say, for the sake of a conservative estimate, we use Minnesota as a model. The North Star State sells licenses to about 120,000 licensed duck hunters each season. Based on the average harvest from the last several years, which was .8 birds per outing and a season harvest of 6.8 birds, we assume the "average hunter" is in the field or on the water 8.5 days. Thus his contribution at $3 per day is, let's say, $24 per season, conservatively. We therefore have more than $2. 8 million generated in one state for one season alone. How much marsh can we buy with that? One helluva lot.

What about Arkansas or Texas, two notable waterfowl states? What income would they generate? Both states enjoy a large supply of avid hunters, long seasons, and people who really care about the duck hunters' lifestyle. I have tentatively titled future projects for these two states the Grand Plan for the Grand Prairies.

The obvious argument is, why does the Grand Plan tax only the public land hunter? The lease hunters don't pay their share, nor do guys who may not lease, but hunt private lands by permission. Well, according to my Grand Plan, the lease hunters, the duck club guy, saltwater sea duck chasers, and permission askers are not exempt. They have to pay the daily fee as well. Even though lease hunters are renting lands that are managed for ducks it is still in their best interest to contribute. Why? you ask. Because this plan will work so well that in a few short years, there will be so much fantastic marshland to hunt that will be open to the public, lease values and club memberships will drop in price due to the competition from excellent public hunting land that will be made available through the Grand Plan tax. This is simple economics. Why would a group of hunters pay for a lease when public areas will be less crowded and there will be more quality duck hunting available for all? The small daily fee will pay huge dividends for the public hunter, the lease-holder, and the duck club devotee.

The formula for Grand Plan purchases will be based upon urgency—due to possible drainage or development—or proximity to heavily hunted public areas. The first scenario will be accomplished by hunters calling the Grand Plan hot-line, where they will be able to report a planned shopping mall development or even something as simple as seeing a farmer purchasing large-diameter pipe down at the building supply store. Unless said farmer is in an oil-producing area and is moving crude from one spot to another, it is likely that if he is buying pipe he is draining potholes. Dial the Grand Plan hotline, and the duck hunting real estate agents will move in to make an offer on the spot. Or if a duck hunter is driving to work and happens to see a couple of guys in hard hats out measuring and looking at a piece of wetland, again, dial the hotline and the Grand Plan agents will move in for a land grab. Further, hunters calling in these tips will be rewarded cash prizes and hunting equipment from the Grand Plan coffers, which will provide incentive for all hunters to keep their eyes open for more opportunities.

In the case of heavily hunted areas, duck hunters will be surveyed annually. They will be required to log on to the Grand Plan Web site, where they'll be encouraged to vote for the most overhunted, overcrowded, idiot-filled public hunting situations they have encountered over the last season. Grand Plan biologists and agents will target the top 100 areas each year, and they will buy as much land as possible in proximity to these areas, creating more public hunting land, and in many cases expanding the acreage tenfold. This will immediately alleviate the felt hunting pressure, while also vastly improving the hunting, as the birds will have resting areas that did not exist before.

In fact, the Grand Plan system will work so well that in a matter of approximately three years, there will be no poor public hunting areas, and there will be plenty of elbowroom for all. Sky busters and pass shooters as we know them today will become an endangered species, shunned by all who support the Grand Plan and its doctrine. More important, there will be no need for uneducated hunters to attempt to pass-shoot ducks working another spread of decoys, or take eighty-yard shots at passing geese, as has been witnessed by many in hunting public areas over the years. Since there will be so much more open space and hunting opportunity, decoy shooters will have plenty of space to ply their trade properly. Ducks will be properly shot—over decoys all the time, by every duck hunter. Those hunters who do not have the financial means to participate in decoy shooting, but who might be able to participate in the Grand Plan by paying the daily fees required, will be eligible for long-term, low-interest loans so they can buy a simple spread of decoys, along with a boat and a motor.

As an integral part of the plan, insurance for any duck-related property or area will also be offered. The plan will likewise protect Grand Plan property holdings with insurance. This will be the Abuser and Sign Shooter arm of the plan, or A. S. S. A small portion of the funds raised through duck hunters' daily fees will go to maintaining an insurance policy to be used to improve all wetlands and fringe areas in case of vandalism or abuse. For example, if Billy Pete shoots a hole in the bottom of Stinky's pirogue, the insurance does not cover this mishap. Stinky should find someone else to hunt with, even if Billy Pete is his brother-in-law. If, however, Stinky finds that some lower-than-pond-scum loser has defaced a sign at a Waterfowl Production Area, that sign will be replaced through funds collected via the Grand Plan. Further, the Grand Plan will hire only those contractors who are serious duck hunters to do such repair work. Thus, mandatory participation by duck hunters in the Grand Plan will benefit everyone, again by having some of their moneys returned to them via their day jobs. In the same vein, real estate agents who will be buying marshland for the Grand Plan network will also have to be duck hunters. These real estate agents will have their purchases approved by Grand Plan biologists. The normal commission enjoyed by agents will be reduced to benefit the overall program. Bankers involved in the boat-and-motor or decoy loan program will also be required to be duck hunters. Grand Plan contractors will not be required to participate in Grand Plan projects during the open waterfowl season in their state.

To avoid fraudulent claims by contractors, agents, or anyone associated or hired by the Grand Plan who claims to be a serious duck hunter, the Grand Plan staff will conduct spousal interviews of said vendor, and spouses will be questioned on all facets of the potential vendor's affliction for ducks or geese. If there is not sufficient spousal grumbling, and grousing about dog hair on good furniture; development of ear canal damage from high-balled, Arkansas-style calls in the cellar; evidence of decoy trailers parked in the yard; and/or determination that duck hunting has caused significant hardship in terms of marital bliss, the contract will not be awarded to said vendor.

The Grand Plan staff is currently involved in research on how to collect funds at public hunting areas, since stationing an employee at each marsh or pothole across the nation will be prohibitively expensive. Punched cards are a possibility, and license vendors, who would punch the card for the following morning, could sell them. Merchants would be happy to handle the punched cards as a lost leader item, since every duck hunter would have to stop the evening before the next day's hunt; the sales of gloves, ammunition, Slim Jims, and other necessities would increase due to increased hunter traffic. Like baseball cards, collectible punched cards would feature the photo of a prominent Grand Plan duck hunter on the face, with his shooting statistics and valuable tips on the reverse. Hunters would no doubt enjoy these entertaining tidbits of information. Imagine... "Since Jim changed to the Beretta with a little more cast-off, he knows he'll shoot better, giving him the confidence to keep his face down in the blind when the ducks make the final pass. His overall gadwall hitting percentage has gone up to .664."

Thus far, the only reasonable solution in terms of collection has come in the form of contacting soft drink distributors or video game vendors who are dyed-in-the-wool duck hunters—asking them to participate in the plan by placing electronic collection boxes on select fence posts in hunting areas, near boat ramps and trails through bogs, and in parking areas. The anticipated problem with this system, however, is the technology in the dollar bill readers. They are finicky to use, and, of course, the majority of duck hunters will be trying to use them in the dark.

Eventually, as the Grand Plan takes hold, it is likely that in five to ten years, virtually all of the prime wetlands available in North America will be under the Grand Plan's management. This will, of course, necessitate expansion of the program into Phase Two, which will develop duck hunting habitat where it does not currently exist. For example, Pennsylvania is a state that is heavily populated by citizens who yearn for duck hunting, evidenced by the fact that the Keystone State sells more than 100,000 waterfowl licenses each year. However, in this heavily forested environment, relatively few waterfowl opportunities exist. Thus, Phase Two will call for the seasonal flooding of the lower elevations of Pennsylvania to create a northern tier of flooded timber habitat that does not currently exist. Pennsylvania will then enjoy the famous Arkansas-style green timber hunting, which will open up huge new hunting areas, provide new jobs for duck guides, and revitalize the duck hunting industry in the East. Arkansas residents should note, however, that Pennsylvania's new duck mecca would not impact Arkansans seriously, since cold weather will inevitably drive the ducks south at some point each year.

Phase Two will, however, affect the orange-clad legion of deer hunters in Pennsylvania, and may cause something of a ruckus if the water levels are raised too high. Ideally, the Grand Plan would put just enough water in the valleys to encourage good duck hunting, but leave the mountaintops free for deer hunters to ply their trade. Alternatively, the Grand Plan will have reserve funds to form a militia to battle the deer hunters, but the Grand Planners do not wish to start a turf war. This will be especially true in battling the deer hunters who, in addition to owning large numbers of very accurate rifles, will be plenty riled up and very jealous of all duck hunters, who will be enjoying all the riches and benefits that the Grand Plan will provide.

New Mexico will be targeted by Grand Plan Planners for a future project, as there simply is not enough water in this state, and thus there exists terrific duck hunting potential that is wasting away. Grand Planners envision an elaborate system of dikes throughout eastern New Mexico, combined with cornfield plantings and other habitat improvements. The epicenter of the project will be Roswell. The residents of Roswell have supposedly cultivated relationships with extraterrestrial beings, and a surefire way to bring new recruits to the sport of duck hunting is to plan ahead and get them from other planets. To mix alien and baseball metaphors, as was said in arguably the best baseball movie of all time, *Field of Dreams*, "If you build it, they will come."

Canada will be a future expansion site for the Grand Plan, where it will be known as That Grand Plan, Eh? Thousands of outdoor hockey rinks exist in small towns throughout Canada, and every one of them can be easily modified to hold water through important nesting and breeding months each spring. This opportunity is just lying there, waiting for action.

There is much work to be done, and for the time being the Grand Plan is short on staff, this being a one-man show at this stage, and that one man is busy taking his kids to ball games and daydreaming in church. But in the not-too-distant future you may know the plan is working when you roll your hunting rig up to a boat ramp in the fog of the predawn some morning and see a figure hunched over in the darkness, trying to iron a dollar bill by running it back and forth over the gunwale of a decoy-filled boat. Cursing, he'll be trying to get a last dollar into the little money collection station, and after five or six tries, when the dollar reader has spit the bill out repeatedly, he will realize that George Washington should be facing up, not down. That person will be me. I've never had much luck getting those dollar readers to work, and now that I think about it, maybe the honor system would work better anyway.

Chapter Eighteen

WRITTEN RECORDS

I nspired by the practices of some of the great duck clubs of yesteryear, I have always felt it was important that our duck club keep a logbook. Almost surprisingly, our little group has now strung together twenty-odd years of chasing ducks more or less successfully. At least we are successful in chasing them. Whether or not the chasing is consecrated by photographs of happy hunters laden under weighty duck straps is another story. We seem to be long on the spirit of the chase, and we are determined. We are short on old photos, gone yellow with age, bound into the pages of our gunning log. I do have a photo of Charlie and me, with a limit of blue-bills apiece, stuck to the refrigerator with a magnet. It isn't a very pithy display in an old-world context, but it means a lot to me, and I see the refrigerator door more often than I'd see a dusty old book. In short, ours is a group more apt to swap tales over a beer on the tailgate than over brandy in the library. I, for one, thought that was why it was called a tailgate. None of us has a library, although I do have a library card. I digress.

The Dubay Lake Club, as we call it, will be noted in the annals of duck hunting history in this country as *Petticoat Junction* is likely to be remembered as one of the high works of Hollywood. We do have a motto, "Don't Shoot the Decoys." This regal code I planned to translate into Latin and embroider on shirts and caps and beer can coolers. I thought the Latin motto might be an elegant touch, sort of our own *E Pluribus Unum* deal. But it seems that at the time Latin was widely spoken, nobody was using shotguns, or decoys, so it didn't translate well. We have been a little hesitant to just put the motto on our belongings in the King's English. It just seemed like it might be a little too obvious to anyone who knows much about the rudiments of the sport. You know, don't shoot at the damned decoys! It's hard on them. It makes them sink. This is part of a little internal problem we have at the club.

Let's just say that the history recorded in our logbooks notes not only the antics of three men, and later a boy or two as well, but the care, feeding, repairing, misplacing, and finding of various dogs, boats, motors, decoys, suspect vehicles, and canoes, and an ever changing palette of marshes, lakes, ponds, potholes, and the occasional picked field.

We had a rough start. We agreed early on that a fancy leather-bound logbook was a little pretentious for us as a group, and in the early years our records were kept on a tablet. We didn't even have a clubhouse for the log to live in, and we worked out of a storage shed behind Charlie's house, where we kept boats and decoys and had kennels attached.

Sadly, the records from our first season were lost, as they were converted into the lining for a mouse nest, which appeared in one of the decoy bags the next spring. The following year our resident veterinarian, Dick, was elected to solve the mouse problem by virtue of his higher education in the habits of the animal world. He hung the tablet on a nail so the critters couldn't reach it.

✦ ✦ ✦

Over the years, the entries that stand out in our very informal gunning log are not the days of driving snow and diving ducks charging over our decoys, or the perfect retrieves through rolling waves, but the asides that are recorded along with grocery lists and to-do lists that adorn the pages. Looking back over twenty years, our books reflect that we did kill some ducks, but the duck killing stands out as nothing more than the conduit that lets the rest of the stuff that has happened happen.

There is a listing from a decade or so ago when—on a freezing November day, the last of the season that year before the ice signaled the end of our hunting—I recorded seeing a large fire in the distance at approximately ten in the morning. I rowed across the lake and jumped in the truck, fearing as I went that it was Charlie's house that was on fire. I knew he was off at work, but the location on the horizon put the column of black smoke in close proximity. Careering down a gravel road, I came to a blazing house fire, and after skidding to a stop, learned with great relief that the local volunteer fire station had set fire to an abandoned farmhouse as a training exercise. I recall going off to a convenience store to load my thermos with soup, and the log shows I killed two goldeneyes and saw an amazing migration of tundra swans later that day.

Charlie has an entry noted from about the same era, mentioning nothing about the weather or shooting or decoys. At that time he had a big German shorthaired pointer that was one of the most versatile of that breed of versatile dogs. He was truly a dog for all seasons—pointing, retrieving, and hunting as hard as any dog of any breed I have ever seen. The dog's name was Dutch, and we lovingly referred to him as the Dutchman, even though he could be a sandwich-stealing, shoe-chewing, chase-me-around-the-yard-to-get-your-duck-call-back cocksure kind of dog. He didn't so much impress you with style as he frustrated you with attitude. Charlie's entry reads, "On the walk back to the vehicle, the Dutchman located a raccoon in a trap, which was fastened inside a twelve-foot section of corrugated drainpipe. The Dutchman entered the pipe. A donnybrook ensued. Final score: Dutchman 1, Raccoon 0."

Several years back, there were several entries inside of a week that noted morning shoots for teal, wood ducks, and other species. After duck hunting entries, either Dick or Charlie added, "Heard a rooster pheasant cackle by the boat landing," or "There was a pheasant behind the south blind about ten o'clock." Then, the next day, "I heard the pheasant again." The following weekend, Charlie wrote:

Temperature about 48 degrees, wind from the southeast, so son Jeff and I hunted the south blind...about forty decoys. We had a little flurry of wood ducks at first light, and I called two mallards about 8:30 and killed the drake. Easy retrieve for Janny. At 9:15, I was standing up in the blind when I heard the pheasant again, as he flew right across the lake from the north. Get this—straight at the blind at eye level. Needless to say it was a kamikaze flight. Another easy retrieve for Janny.

From three years ago, another entry from Charlie is titled "The Day I Should Have Stayed in Bed":

Arrived at the lake on time. Wind north at twenty, sky overcast—perfect day. Half way to the north blind I discovered that I was ankle deep in Dubay Lake water. No plug. (Bad words said aloud). Should have checked it. Went back to the south side and made a plug from a whittled stick and a rag. No longer on time. Threw out a dozen decoys, and morning flight commenced. Missed a single bluebill with my first shot, and my new gun would not cycle the second shell into the chamber. (More bad words said aloud.) This has been happening all season, as you all know and have reminded me on numerous occasions. I waited until almost ten o'clock, and killed one more bluebill. Decided to fix gun problem once and for all. Left decoys out, since have the whole day off, and will return later. Crossed lake quickly, and emptied a few gallons from boat. Got in truck and went to Ray's gun shop. He produced the manual for my gun. I had put one of the sleeves in backwards. (Bad words said under breath in place of business.) "Should be fine now," claimed Ray. Drove out county road by the empty corncrib. Shot gun three times in a row—twice. All better. Drove back toward the lake, and a mile short of landing, wheel fell off truck. Just fell off. Truck looked like a three-legged dog. (Screamed bad words-jumped up and down in road, and kicked truck.) Walked to gray house and called tow truck. Walked rest of way to lake and sat in the blind until sunset. Saw some geese but did not shoot anything else. Walked back to gray house to call for a ride to the house. All out of bad words, bought beer on the way home."

Of course, not all of the log entries are so wearisome. Dick, the vet, recorded an entry on a day we still talk about.

October 20. Road trip yielded a flooded soybean field across the road from our small pothole near Litchfield. There were six inches of water in a low spot that covered about one acre, and all of the beans were knocked down. We saw the spot from the road with binoculars first. You could not have gotten one more green-wing teal on that piece of water without a pry bar. I had Charlie with me, and we flushed the birds off without shooting, and we put just three decoys down. We both lay on the ground—me on my back, and Charlie and his ample girth on his stomach. He shoots pretty good like that when he is pointed in the right direction. We shot and shot and got our birds, and killed two geese that came to us too. What a day. All the better since it was warm and sunny, and we were sure we were going to be shut out.

And another that was memorable in its own right.

November 11. Clear, 36 degrees, thick ice around the edges out five yards on average. Light north wind. Two of us in the blind today with one brown dog. The Good Lord opened up the duck gates today, but apparently he did not open them very far, as only buffleheads were small enough to slip through. Steady stream from a half hour after sunrise until we finished up—out of bullets at about ten. Doug only had fifteen shells to start with, and I had not many more, plus three spare goose loads in my coat. The little ducks were sliding across the decoys at about thirty yards—faster than jackrabbits on skates—and would then flare over the end of the spread. We shot them on the flare. All drakes but two. We did get five apiece, with one goose load left-over. Took a lot of photos of pretty white drakes. Watched Vikings at Green Bay while cleaning them. Vikings play like we shoot.

One of my favorites is written in my hand. It was from the mid-80s, on a year when a long summer drought had left the Dubay club's waters very low.

October 19. West wind, 45 degrees, partly cloudy. Alone today. Everyone else working this morning. No work at the store for me until afternoon, so put out six dozen mallard decoys, plus pintails, wood ducks, three floater geese. I put about a dozen on the new mud bar in front of the blind, and could wade all the decoys out. A first for me in ten years on Dubay. Shot one wood duck for two barrels at the first bell, and then sat. Saw ten geese—they did not even look at me. I suspect they are using the Sundance golf course; maybe a guy would do better in plaid slacks than in camouflage? With west wind, could hear the highway and trains on the tracks all morning. A single drake pintail surprised me midmorning. By the time I got to him, he was at the outside edge of the decoys, going away. I shot, and almost to my surprise he fell stone dead. It seemed as if the whole episode happened in slow motion. I rowed out to retrieve him, and the surface of the water was perfectly calm, save a slight ripple pushed by the boat. A mature bull sprig lay on his side in the water with a small droplet of blood on the side of his face, just below his eye. It looked as if he was out of a Carlson still life. He was perfect—gray, white, and caramel, on a background of pea green translucence. I can still see him in that same spot, floating high on the water, not a feather out of place.

I suppose that recalling the memories of triumph and folly is why men choose to record the details of hunting as we have all these years. Our series of tattered tablets and spiral notebooks hung on a nail on the wall of a shed record our favorite portions of life and the rich pageant of the fall migration in the same way men painted on the walls of caves to record their hunting history. However, as I age, it becomes increasingly clear to me that the recording is less and less important, and the reflecting takes on more meaning. As Louis Armstrong once said of jazz, "If you gotta ask, you'll never know."

Chapter Nineteen

WILD ROSE COUNTRY

On a bitter night in February or looking at the parched, brown lawn from my porch swing in August—both times when it seems another duck season will never come—I often catch myself reminiscing about the really great hunts I have made, and special places or moments that made them so memorable. It seems I am always trying to keep a little glow on the duck hunting fire that lives inside me all year. It is somewhat like the man who uses the euphemism "between opportunities" for being out of work, I always feel that, no matter how long a period of time there is between them, I'm between duck hunts. When I do this reminiscing, I often think back to a trip I made some years ago in Alberta, and a mallard hunt that plays in my mind like it was stored on a movie reel.

First off, I love everything about Canada. I love Canadians, and hockey, and the Calgary Stampede, and money with loons on it. I love the accommodating style that allows most Canadians to turn a statement into a question by adding "eh?" to the end of a sentence. I love open spaces, and big rolling grainfields, wind generators, k. d. lang music, and the sight of a row of combines, distinguished only by their headlights, moving through a wheat field in the dark. I love the big mountains and the masculine steelhead rivers of British Columbia, and the more refined salmon rivers of the Maritimes. Calgary, Alberta, wins the vote for my favorite airport, and I like downtown Edmonton, the maple leaf centered on the flag, and Labatts beer. I can honestly say I have never had a bad experience in Canada or an untoward incident of any kind. Canada is paradise for me, and perhaps that is why I often remember it so fondly.

I have made countless forays north over the years, beginning with fishing trips launched from the native Minnesota of my youth. Each August my family would load the wood-sided station wagon and point it north through the pine and birch and red sand country of the northern part of the North Star State, en route to the cooler, simpler summer life in Canada.

With the car windows wide open and the summer air blasting into the back seat, my siblings and I would squirm and fight over cool drinks as we passed garish Paul Bunyan billboards and roadside stands hawking Indian moccasins near towns like Sauk Rapids, and Brainerd and Black Duck. Even at that young age I had developed an elitist bias for Canada. I saw those billboards and stands as false prophets—I believed the real wilderness began a little farther north, when the resort signs, with their jumping walleyes and promises of free ice and color television, disappeared.

I recall reaching the Canadian border on those trips of long ago and feeling as if it were the gateway to a land of much grander scale, as if by passing through the gates to Ontario, we left the heat of the highway and all that was mundane behind us. In Canada we were better, more self-sufficient people. We refreshed in the shade and smells of huge pines, kept house in our simple cabin, and skirted the rock outcroppings and islands of huge, blue lakes in our aluminum boats, while lobbing flatfish and Hawaiian wigglers into the dark lairs of smallmouth bass and northern pike, or trolled leeches or night crawlers for golden walleyes.

I had the same feeling of living on a grander scale late on a dark Sunday, just before Halloween, when I found myself parked on a bluff over the Peace River in northern Alberta, while I looked hundreds of feet down toward the river below. The sky virtually oozed by in folds and creases of heavy, gray cloud, leaving me with the impression that I was closer to the clouds than I was to the black surface of the water far beneath me. It was an hour before sunset, but I could still see for miles across the wheat fields and could make out silos and farms and water towers in the distance.

I had taken up residence near the Peace River Valley for a number of days and found it easy, despite the tardiness of the season this far north, which was just a couple of good stone's throws from the Northwest Territories. I was able to shoot

Canada geese almost anywhere I could find a concentration of birds and could get permission to shoot the field they were using. I was having a marvelous time, and all week there were plenty of birds on the move. Each day would begin with skeins of perfect little Canada geese crossing the sky after a long sunrise. Many geese had just arrived from the tundra country a day's flight north. Decked out in rich browns and black and stark white, most flocks of geese were predominantly birds of the year, and they literally fell out of the sky to get into my wheat stubble decoy sets. But the reason the geese are easy here is because these are the very first grainfields many of these birds see after leaving the summer nesting country in the high Arctic, and they are the first grainfields any of the juvenile birds have ever seen. I recall a number of occasions when, at midmorning, a high flock would appear in the sky, and they'd set tired wings from hundreds and hundreds of yards away, gliding towards the decoys after an all-night flight from the tundra. It would seem like it took hours for them to come down to decoy level. Goose shooting aside, however, I was having trouble finding the ducks, or more specifically, getting the kind of duck hunting I was looking for.

The area north of the town of Peace River and stretching up to Fort Vermillion and High Level is a mix of pine stands laid out in square grids, interspersed with huge, rolling agricultural areas planted in endless fields of peas and wheat. Many of these fields are miles square, ending only to accommodate a county road, railroad line, pothole, or good-sized creek draw, which at this time of year shine with yellow-topped aspens. There are small lumber operations here, with their smoking kilns, grain elevators, family farms, and large collective farms tended by the Mennonites. The Mennonite farms are easily recognizable by the sheer size of the housing facilities, which often stand as orderly as barracks, or by the cleanliness of the farmstead itself. You'll never see more impeccable farms, with straight fences, rows and rows of plastic-wrapped silage bales, fresh paint, and sparkling machinery. Beyond these farms, more grainfields stretch to the horizon.

Oftentimes it is not the horizon that stops the endless, rolling fields of wheat. Many end at the banks of the Peace River itself, where sheer bluffs fall hundreds of feet to the river churning below. The Peace is the only cut through the gently rolling farmland that surrounds it, and it appears as a deep gouge, giving the impression that the whole of the till-able land is perched upon the edge of a precipice—both sides teetering near the edge of the majestic river below. Bridges, sandbars, and the huge white-tailed deer that roam this part of Alberta often appear far beneath me, and if I get too close to the edge I'm left with the same vertigo I feel high in a city skyscraper, watching people and traffic below. Many times I am able to look down into the river valley to see flocks of ducks and geese trading the river underneath the lip of the bluffs or banks that I stand on, but it has seemed—for the last few days on this trip—that when I am on the west bank, the

ducks fly up and over the east side. By the time I guess their whereabouts, it is too dark to follow them. Or after crossing the river, I lose my way and am not able to reconnect with the birds I saw earlier.

On this dark afternoon, I watched the dark skies and followed a few small flocks of ducks to little marshes, but as the wind blew cold through the window of my rented van, I was content to wait until the morning. I knew where there were likely limits of gadwall and wigeon and pintail to be had in small potholes, but I was really looking for a stubble shoot, where I could decoy mallards over dry land. This is one of my favorite ways to hunt and decoy ducks, and this is why I came. I want to get underneath the big, late-migrating ducks that are the last and best of the migration, before they work their way south to the grain that lies in the true prairie of southern Alberta or Saskatchewan. I decided to skip goose hunting altogether the next morning so that I could look for ducks full-time.

After the day dawned cold and clear, I assumed the slate gray clouds of the previous day had been blown out by high pressure, but another dark front loomed across the western horizon and the morning sun was nothing more than a breather between two systems. Still, the sun was warm enough that I peeled off my jacket and cracked the window as I pulled out of the drive to head back down the east side of the Peace to look for a field and for dryland mallards.

Two hours and a thermos later, I had crawled the van down thirty of forty miles of gravel road parallel to the river and looked at countless acres of land. There was windblown snow on the ground and little drifts built up along the bottom of the wire fences. I saw a big white-tailed buck, his antlers appearing as white as elephant tusks in the gray light as he trotted, head high, across a plowed field. The only vehicle I met on the gravel was the empty school bus, and the driver waved with two fingers as he passed. I saw a number of flights of geese, a few small knots of ducks, and some swans, but I was resigning myself to the fact that I was going to have to turn back and head toward some pothole country with a bag of floaters if I wanted to get any duck shooting. However, while turning the van around in a pullout that granted access to a stout grain silo, I saw five mallards swing over a line of aspens just over the river, which was out of sight, but only several hundred yards away.

Then I saw three more big ducks, then two more, then a flock of thirty or so settled behind the trees. I parked on a little rise in the road, flipping the motor off so I could see through my binoculars without the vibration of the engine. I could not see any more ducks, and all I could see through the trees was what appeared to be a rumpled field that was about half covered in snow. I saw another duck or two, and then twenty mallards circled low over the field, swung over it again, and dropped in.

I couldn't see where the ducks where coming from, but I knew it was not very far, since I never saw a duck higher then thirty or forty yards off the ground. These were not new migrants. I scratched my head, reset my cap, and continued to scan the skies, looking well up into the gray, and far up and down the area that I knew was just over the river itself. Then I saw three more ducks, just over the aspen trees, and they fell right into the spot. I knew from some experience that ducks landing in a field never just fall into a spot on dry land unless there are a substantial number of ducks already on the ground. There had to be a pretty good group of birds on the ground in there somewhere. I elected to abandon my vigil of monitoring the field, and fired up the van to go and seek out some permission.

Two miles back from the direction I had come was a small, pale blue farmhouse, flanked by assorted machinery that included a big John Deere tractor, a Dodge muscle car up on blocks, and two dead snow machines in the front yard. I pulled in, knocked, and was met by a young man in his early thirties who was wearing coveralls and socks. He explained that he was just heading back out the door after lunch. I stood in his little mudroom, and he explained that the field across the road was indeed his. It was only about sixty acres, and sort of an odd shape since it was a slim rectangle, pinched in on the east and west sides between the road and the river and surrounded on all four sides by tall poplars and aspens.

"What is not slim in that field is the mud, eh?" he continued, seemingly pleased to have someone to talk with. "I stuck a combine in there, oh I guess two weeks ago now. As it was, I don't think I finished two passes along the west side of the field anyway, eh? There is a spring hole or something in it. You can't see it through the windbreak, but the whole field is full of wheat. I will probably lose the whole thing at this stage. The snow has knocked it down, and them ducks are in there eating it too, eh? I heard a lot of ducks coming over the house a couple nights last week, quacking and chattering. Someone might as well eat it I guess, eh? You wanna shoot some of those ducks? You go ahead, and have fun."

I thanked him profusely, and left the driveway feeling the broad smile cross my face that my wife tells me I wear only when I have fallen into something very, very good. The icing on the cake was the farmer telling me to "have fun." No landowner has ever said that to me in the States. They usually tell me to be very, very careful, or not to shoot near the horses. Another item to add to my list of reasons to love Canada. Then I thought to myself, this guy lives well up the road, and he is hearing ducks headed to that field in the night? This would appear to be a serious mallard buildup. Behind the wheel again, I rubbed my hands together in anticipation, then parked in the pullout near the silo again to eat some of my packed lunch. Then I closed my eyes for a few minutes.

It was after three o'clock in the afternoon by the time I blinked awake from my short siesta, and the southwest wind had grown to a steady twenty miles per hour. Getting the decoy bag strapped on my back, and wearing my muddy, white laboratory coat as my snow camouflage, I walked into the field as a little sleet began to spit intermittently. The field was wet, and once I got through the windbreak of aspens and poplars I could see why the field had looked so rumpled. It was a sea of unharvested wheat, and it lay all askew, with large patches of snow riding atop it like white foam on breaking waves. I tried to be fast and quiet, although the decoys on my back made a *schlep, schlep* sound for every step I took. Then the duck heads popped up in unison, and for an instant I had the feeling that I had tried to disarm a bomb and had just cut the wrong wire. Ducks exploded out of the field. I'm not particularly skilled in estimating numbers of ducks on the wing, but to say there were two solid acres of mallards would not be an exaggeration.

I readjusted my backpack and walked, adrenaline aided, to the spot where the ducks had been the thickest. I could see the huge black scars in the field that told the tale of a struggle between mud and machinery, including the flattened tracks left by the heavy Caterpillar it took to pull the farmer's combine free. The spot where the ducks had been was flattened as well, literally trampled by waterfowl. In roughly the middle of the field it resembled a little arena, with flat ground, and traces of snow and black dirt, circled by higher borders of rolling wheat topped with snow. I set out three dozen duck shells and silhouettes, and folded and ramped up some wheat as a place to lie comfortably. I fashioned a pillow from my shell bag and empty decoy bag. Already groups of twos and threes were trying to circle—wings intermittently set—back to the spread. But before I got to the business at hand, I wanted to have a look at the river and see just where these ducks had been coming from. I ducked through the line of aspens that lined the edge of the bluff over the Peace, and a hundred feet below me was a huge backwater formed by a sandbar—in the shape of Florida and maybe a half mile in length. The backwater was black with ducks, and I kept myself hidden while I snapped off a number of photos of birds preening and sleeping on the water, and standing on the snow-dusted sandbar.

As I returned to my decoy spread, four big mallards blasted out. I thumbed three shells into my gun, then closed the bolt with a clang and prepared to welcome the next group. I realized that I had not been able to see the ducks coming onto the field from the road since they were not coming onto the field—they had been flying off the river and up the side of the bluff, and once they crested the edge of the bank, they just dropped over the trees and into the wheat.

A group of thirty mallards appeared over the trees, and—hens chattering—the whole group locked wings for the short descent to my spread. I let the first bird, a drake, flare for landing almost at ground level. I picked a greenhead above me, and touched off my first shot. He crumpled, as did a hen that was just above him—a "Scotch double." I giggled to myself: *Not only am I covered up in ducks, but now I'm shooting them two at a crack.* At the very least, I was carefully following the farmer's instructions to "have fun."

I could have filled out the liberal Alberta duck limit in about four minutes, but I stretched things out to just short of half an hour by picking drakes—save the hen I dropped by luck or accident with my first salvo. I thought to myself that invariably the saddest part about a great hunt is that if it is truly great, it is over just as fast as it began.

While I picked up decoys in the rapidly fading light, more and more ducks poured into other parts of the field. In no hurry to leave, I bagged my silhouettes, then wandered around the field a little just to soak everything in. I was amazed to find that, as it grew darker, I was able to walk up to within just five or ten feet of a number of wild mallards—close enough to touch them as they fed voraciously in and almost under the waves of wheat. In the near dark they would feed, and then flutter up like barnyard chickens, coming to rest just yards away, where they would resume feeding. It was likely that a number of these ducks, fresh from the far north, had never seen a human before, and were as wild and pure a creature as I would ever encounter. I have never before or since been so close to totally wild birds in such great numbers.

My flashlight beam caught the rearview mirror of the rented van as I neared it, and going around to the back doors I shed my bag, coats, and duck strap. I sat on the back bumper and opened a Labatts, then flipped off the dome light so my eyes could adjust to the dark all around me. Sitting in the cold night air, I could hear ducks above me, chattering as they went into the field in the dark. The yard light from the farmer's house was the only landmark visible on an otherwise black horizon. After a few minutes I loaded things into the back, and smiled as I looked down to read the license plate. It read "Alberta," and underneath the larger registration numbers, "Wild Rose Country." Maybe they should change it to "Wild Duck Country." A very pleasant thought as I drove off into the dark Canadian night.

Chapter Twenty

CLOSE ENOUGH

I had the opportunity to hunt ducks with a youngster this year, and frankly I had forgotten just how much fun duck hunting was when I was a youth. It is a time when vigor can overwhelm reason; when brute strength helps overcome ice, thick cattails, or floating bogs; and when enthusiasm keeps watch over the skies long after a reasonable chance to decoy birds has faded away. More important, in duck hunting, kids get by on less sleep. I'm not all that great a shot now, but sharing a blind with a youngster made me recall the days when killing a duck from a flock of decoying birds was more a possibility than a probability. Remember those days? When your first question to the adult who was hunting with you was, "Did you shoot too?" Or, "Did I get him?" If you have ever introduced someone to hunting, you know there is only one answer to the latter question, and it's perfectly OK if it's a white lie. Being with this young man recalled some great days in my own youth, and it also made me pause to consider what he has to look forward to, and what my own children may have to look forward to in a world that seems to get less and less wild every day.

I say "youngster," but Jeff is seventeen already, so he doesn't need me to cut up his dinner for him. In fact he's big for seventeen: shy, very polite—a high school hockey player who eats like he has a tapeworm. He wears no tattoos that I can see and lacks the nose ring I see on some of his peers, and his hair is cut above the ears. Disparage me for the stereotyping if you want, but I am so tired of the pale waifs who serve me coffee at Starbucks. They hand me the cup of coffee I just paid for like a prison inmate slipping his empty tray out of a slot in the door. These grungy skateboarders and white suburban rapper kids with blue hair and matted goatees—all they want is for someone to sponsor them at one extreme sport or another. You want an extreme sport, kid? How about bluebill hunting on a lake that is making ice in late November? The boat ride alone can be more frightening than any skateboard ramp, and your blue skin will match your hair when it's over. Or hunt down in Arkansas in some of that flooded timber. Running the outboard through the stumps in the dark is plenty of challenge—don't hit any and you get to keep your teeth.

Anyway, part of the reason I like Jeff so much is that he's so normal. That doesn't mean I only want to hunt with straight-laced folks. I'm not Pat Boone either. But the old saw that opposites attract doesn't fly in the duck blind.

Jeff is the son of one of my best hunting friends, and I have appreciated his company this year. Jeff also appeared to enjoy the chance to get out a few extra days when his Dad was forced to keep his nose to the working grindstone. Although he is just a budding duck caller, Jeff is one of the best rowers of duck boats I have ever come across. With a little more work, he could be great, perhaps the best the upper Midwest has ever seen. I tell him that often, as I have always heard it is important to lavish children with praise and positive reinforcement. I am grooming him in case there is ever a specific competition for rowing camouflaged aluminum skiffs. He practices taking me, and our mountain of gear, back and forth across our marsh at every opportunity. For extra practice, and to keep him a step ahead of any other developing skiff rowers, I also like to send him back and forth across the marsh whenever I need another jacket or forget my thermos at the truck.

The surveys say that our hunting ranks are getting older and older, that there are fewer children and families participating in hunting in general, and that, in the long run, lack of participation will be what hurts the outdoor sports the most. I believe it, based on the casual conversations I have with other hunters, and on advertisements and Internet posts I see. A lot of the talk and frustration is from fathers, searching for a quality hunting experience for their children; the kind of experience they enjoyed as kids. Reading between the lines, much of the frustration felt by many stems from the fact that, as our society moves farther and farther from its rural roots—as land is being tied up and developed—it is becoming tougher and tougher for a father to introduce a son or a daughter to shooting or fishing, unless they are firmly rooted in the sport already. The Take a Kid Hunting mantra is becoming a more and more popular chant, and we'd best take it seriously. If we don't lead and develop future outdoorsmen and -women right now, there will be so little outdoors left it won't matter.

I think about what it would take for Jeff to get started duck hunting if he didn't have a father and a "support group" of a couple of other adults to ease him into the sport. First there is the realm of public hunting. Public ground may still be a viable option in many plains states and in select areas in the South, but in the West, East and Northeast, public marshes at best offer little chance for a quality experience for adults, much less beginners to the sport. At worst the public areas are crowded, competitive areas where skybusters ply their trade, making the classic decoying bird duck hunt a rarity. Then there is the expense of boats, motors, guns, decoys, license, and stamps, nontoxic shells, waders, and all the other trappings that go with the sport, not to mention guns and a dog or two. All of these things are tough to manage if you are limited to a minimum-wage job and after-school hours.

Not only are there these obstacles, but kids today are often presented with so many options that getting outdoors is lower on the priority list than organized sports, cell phones, home computers, or after-school jobs. In most urban or suburban schools, hunting is frowned upon by faculty and by peers, and guns are more often associated with school violence than with hunting. A trip to the duck or deer camp is no longer the kind of father-son experience that is really welcomed at show-and-tell. It is perhaps tolerated, but hunting is certainly not encouraged, since many students enter their building by passing through a metal detector each day. It's so sad, because hunting and fishing still teach so much that is not about harvesting birds or fish. Being outdoors still teaches what it has always taught—respect, maturity, responsibility, and doing one's share—much in the same way that athletic sports do, but with the weight of responsibility that blood sports carry.

Jeff is lucky that his father hunted, and that he has been encouraged to get involved in the outdoors by his father if it appealed to him. My own father was not a hunter. While I never faulted him for it, when I got the bug, I did everything on my own, reading how-to books and scouring magazines. I made plenty of mistakes as I went along. But I had some school friends who came from hunting families, and I was able to tag along with them in my teens. I also had access to small lakes and farmland, which eliminated one of the biggest obstacles today's kids face. By the time I got the mobility that a driver's license afforded, I was well on my way.

Back when I was Jeff's age, I had permission to hunt a small lake near my home. Maybe sixty acres or so, the water was surrounded by gently rolling cornfields and dirty fence lines. At the north end there was a little bluff split by a dry creek bed, and each bank held a stand of mature oaks and soft maples. In the early weeks of the duck season, these trees would blaze in yellow and maroon and gold—their color vivid against the steel gray water and flat tan of the corn. The lake was oblong in shape, and I hunted a blunt cattail point, precisely at the short top of the western shore, from a borrowed, double-ended boat. I had permission for the entire season, and never saw anyone else hunt the lake.

On a dark morning following a hard overnight frost and a high school football game, I carried my decoys to the little lake against a pressing west wind, sure that the maples would begin to drop some of their brightly colored leaves later in the day. But for now, I was hoping to again meet the mallards and wood ducks that had been arriving shortly after dawn all week. Instead, what greeted me when I arrived was the sound of wooden oars banging lightly against an aluminum boat. A flashlight beam winked as someone set decoys just in front of my point.

Having nowhere else to go, I rushed to my little boat and tried to make the best of my situation. I knew enough to get my back to the wind, but with only a short piece of shoreline to work with, my decision would place me just 100 yards or so down the shoreline from the stranger on "my" point. As I set the first of my decoys, a sarcastic voice bellowed through the dark at me, asking, "Are you sure you're close enough?"

I could feel my face flush, and a tingle of embarrassment rushed down my back. I didn't reply—didn't know what to say. But I set just two more decoys and fairly well rushed back to the shore. Trying mightily to disappear, I parked myself in a makeshift blind in the reeds. I didn't want an argument with a stranger. I was new at this game.

✦ ✦ ✦

As the night sky gave way to the sun, several small flocks came onto the lake. Despite calling and a decoy spread equal to the stranger's, he was the one—not I—who shot several ducks, including a "dead in the air" double on mallards out of a group that had decoyed like they were new to the area. Each time the stranger downed a bird, a dog was sent without fanfare to make the retrieve. Two of the groups that gave him shooting had crossed the fringe of my spread, with wings set. I held fire on both, afraid of a confrontation. I managed a passing shot on a greenhead that was leaving the lake after the stranger had doubled, but that was all of my action for the day.

Once the sun was full up and the flight had stopped, I rowed out to the decoys and retrieved them. When I returned to the shoreline, a stocky man in hip boots waited for me. Sure I was going to receive a lecture, I was slow to pole close to dry land. But as I neared the shoreline, the man reached out to help me beach my little boat, a string of calls swinging out from his chest as he did so. He introduced himself and thanked me for letting the birds work and for not shooting the groups that had just edged my decoys, but had worked his. He offered me two of his ducks.

Half an hour later I was a mile down the road, squeezed into his little kitchen. With ham and eggs and coffee in front of me, I was snug among the toys and dishes and newspapers and bills spread about the room. As I accepted another refill of my coffee, a beautiful little girl toddled into the room in those little feet-attached pajama sleepers kids wear. Her mother followed fast on her heels, and she also carried a new baby, who I learned was just seven weeks old. The stranger was no longer a stranger, and Charlie told me then that they had named the new baby Jeffrey, and as is the wish of a proud father, he hoped some day that Jeffrey would want to go hunting with him. Fortunately, I get to fill in on the days when Charlie has to work.